ENGINEERING AS A
SOCIAL ENTERPRISE

Hedy E. Sladovich, Editor

Papers presented during the 1990 meeting of the National
Academy of Engineering in a symposium dedicated to the memory of
J. Herbert Hollomon

NATIONAL ACADEMY PRESS
Washington, D.C. 1991

NATIONAL ACADEMY PRESS ● 2101 Constitution Avenue, N.W. ● Washington, D.C. 20418

The National Academy of Engineering was established in 1964, under the charter of the National Academy of Sciences, as a parallel organization of outstanding engineers. It is autonomous in its administration and in the selection of its members, sharing with the National Academy of Sciences the responsibility for advising the federal government. The National Academy of Engineering also sponsors engineering programs aimed at meeting national needs, encourages education and research, and recognizes the superior achievements of engineers. Dr. Robert M. White is president of the National Academy of Engineering.

This volume consists of papers and speakers' remarks presented at a symposium entitled "Engineering as a Social Enterprise" during the Twenty-Sixth Annual Meeting of the National Academy of Engineering, 3 October 1990, in Washington, D.C. The interpretations and conclusions expressed in these papers are those of the authors and are not presented as the views of the council, officers, or staff of the National Academy of Engineering.

Library of Congress Card No. 91-61730
International Standard Book No. 0-309-04431-6

Additional copies of this publication are available from:

National Academy Press
2101 Constitution Avenue, N.W.
Washington, D.C. 20418

S-277

Cover: *Römischer Aquädukt*. Painting by Prof. Zeno Diemer. Courtesy of the Deutsches Museum, Munich.

Printed in the United States of America

Planning Committee

Walter G. Vincenti (Symposium Chairman)
Professor Emeritus of Aeronautics and Astronautics
Stanford University

Gerald Nadler
IBM Professor of Engineering Management
Professor and Chairman of Industrial and Systems Engineering
University of Southern California

Walter A. Rosenblith
Institute Professor, Emeritus
Massachusetts Institute of Technology

Rustum Roy
Evan Pugh Professor of the Solid State
Materials Research Laboratory
Pennsylvania State University

Edward Wenk, Jr.
Professor Emeritus of Engineering, Public
    Affairs, and Social Management of Technology
University of Washington

Preface

Engineering is not often thought of as a social enterprise. But in fact social needs and pressures shape what engineers do as much as engineering and technology shape the nature of society. This volume is intended to illuminate some of the ways in which engineers and those they serve—individuals as well as society—must come to understand each other better.

People like J. Herbert Hollomon, a founding member of our Academy, understood such relationships well. He grasped the sociotechnical implications of his time and beyond and acted on his beliefs both as an engineer and as a national leader toward that end. His views on engineering's great challenges presented in 1960 retain much of their relevance and validity today (see appendix for his remarks before a joint meeting of regional engineering groups commemorating National Engineers Week, Schenectady, New York, February 23, 1960). We dedicate this volume of essays, based on presentations given at the 1990 annual meeting symposium "Engineering as a Social Enterprise," to the memory of J. Herbert Hollomon. The symposium marked the close of the 25th anniversary year celebration of the Academy and the establishment of the J. Herbert Hollomon Fellowship, endowed in part through the generous support of the J. Herbert Hollomon Memorial Committee. This fellowship enables the NAE to invite a young person to work at the Academy on policy issues involving significant elements of engineering and technology.

The essays in this volume are based on the proposition that many forces move and shape engineering, technology, culture, and society. They include perspectives on the engineering response to social needs as well as to social forces. There are historical accounts of the relationship between engineering and

v

society, probing examinations of the social forces that determine the engineering agenda, and views on the implications of these forces for the present and future engineering enterprise that reflects, for the most part, the American experience.

Several aspects of the sociotechnical system emerge: the goals and aspirations of individuals as distinct from those of institutions, companies, nations, regions, societies, and the interrelationships between them that operate on many levels and vastly different scales of time and space. These relationships are never static, and engineers and engineering constantly face the challenge of serving both ends of this huge spectrum. Also, the ongoing nature of this change is rapid and complex: interconnections are multiplying exponentially, and the process of social accommodation faces greater and more pervasive tensions. This sometimes results in fast-moving and false directives for technological innovation, as well as constraints on the adoption of new technology by slowly evolving social constructs for adapting and coping with the potential consequences.

Much as engineering achievements reflect the practical use of new knowledge manifested in man-made devices, so they also mirror the evolution and interrelation of engineering, technology, and society. The diversity of made-things is astonishing and goes well beyond necessity and utility alone. They form the visible tip of an iceberg that is the whole sociotechnical system and its processes.

Many people were involved in the preparation of this volume. I would like to thank the symposium speakers for their thoughtful presentations and the symposium planning committee and its chairman Walter Vincenti for their many valuable contributions both in organizing the symposium and in shaping this publication. Special thanks go to Daniel Roos of the Massachusetts Institute of Technology, the J. Herbert Hollomon memorial committee for the means to dedicate this symposium to the memory of J. Herbert Hollomon, and Roland Schmitt and Harvey Brooks for their personal remembrances. As the concluding event in the Academy's 25th anniversary year celebration, the symposium was planned with the oversight of the 25th Anniversary Advisory Committee and additional guidance from the Academy's Advisory Committee on Technology and Society. I also want to recognize Christopher Hill for his comments on the manuscript before publication and members of the NAE Program Office staff under the direction of Bruce R. Guile, including Hedy E. Sladovich, H. Dale Langford, Annmarie Terraciano, and Mary J. Ball, for organizing the symposium and preparing the essays for publication.

ROBERT M. WHITE
President
National Academy of Engineering

Contents

3. PRACTITIONERS' PERSPECTIVES

APPENDIXES

ENGINEERING AS A SOCIAL ENTERPRISE

Introduction

As befits an academy of engineers in concluding the observance of its 25th anniversary, this volume, like the symposium from which it derives, was conceived as an exercise in professional self-education. We hope it will, at the same time, contribute to the wisdom and understanding of readers from the broader community. To both ends, I want here, as best I can, to put the contents of the book into an appropriate conceptual framework. The volume as structured reflects this framework, but making it explicit may be useful.

When the committee charged with planning the symposium met to implement the assigned theme of engineering and society, we quickly found that we shared a common view. Though we expressed it in different words, we agreed that engineering, far from interacting with society from outside as often assumed, is in reality an integral part of the social fabric. Engineering, that is, constitutes a social activity in the same way as do business, government, religion, the fine arts, and the other areas of activity that humans pursue. The sum of these activities, including engineering, makes up what we call society. Thus, the question is not one of engineering *and* society, but engineering *in* society. The committee does not claim any special wisdom for this view. When looked at directly, it is so obvious as to hardly need saying.

Unfortunately—and unproductively—it is not the view that prevails. Most people, I think it fair to say—and I include engineers in "most people"—unconsciously regard engineering as somehow apart from society. Engineering, like technology as a whole, provides good things or terrible problems for the society, but, whatever it is, it takes place somewhere "out there." In a university such as my own, it is something exotic and mysterious that goes on by itself

1

in the school of engineering. In the media, the idea frequently shows up in the phrase "the impact of technology on society" (though, curiously, the impact of society on technology is rarely mentioned). This notion encourages the all-too-frequent image of a technology relentlessly in the driver's seat and outside the checks and balances of the social order.

To what extent this volume succeeds in departing from the stereotype, the reader must judge. Certainly, the symposium on which it is based was put together with that goal in mind. The title of the symposium, "Engineering as a Social Enterprise," was chosen to imply that engineering functions inseparably from the society of which it is a part. To operate within that reality, we need to comprehend better than we do what requirements and constraints are put on engineers by the rest of society and what role the engineer realistically can or should play in that society.

To say that engineering must be seen as an integral part of society is one thing; to analyze it as such, however, is quite another. To think about the problem, we need some kind of mental model, and the stereotypical one of separate entities clearly will not do. A more realistic possibility, which engineers should find congenial, is what has been termed the *sociotechnical system*. Engineers have to deal with systems—technical systems—all the time and are familiar with how they need to be subdivided for analysis. In the sociotechnical model, the entire society is visualized, as we engineers do in our technical work, as a vast integrated system, with the varied social and technical areas of human activity as major interacting subsystems. In this context engineering now appears as one of the subsystems.

As in engineering practice, this subdivision is made so that each subsystem can be analyzed in quasi isolation. Such analysis must be carried out, however—and this is the crucial point—with attention at all times to the interactions between and constraints on the subsystems and to the eventual need to reassemble the system. Such reassembly is essential if the analysis is to be valid and the sociotechnical system is to work. To analyze the subsystems of the total society—industry, business, government, engineering, and so forth—they must be divided in turn into sub-subsystems and subcomponents; these must then be examined individually with an eye again toward reassembly. Engineers are comfortable with such a systems approach.

The initial sociotechnical system, of course, need not be all of society; more usually it will be some functional system within it, such as an airline, hospital, or electric-power network. This sociotechnical system will then have its own social and technical subsystems. Whatever its identity and makeup, however, the initial functional system must operate within the constraints of the overall society. How we organize the analysis in a particular case is a matter of analytical and hierarchical detail. The important thing here is the integrative concept of the sociotechnical system.

The analysis of all of society as a sociotechnical system would obviously be a tall order—and that is clearly a blatant understatement. The difficulty is compounded by the fact that society and its major subsystems are all *adaptive* systems—they change with time in ways that allow them to work better, function more or less at the level they currently do, or at least survive. The overall society adapts to take account of changes originating in its subsystems, and the subsystems adapt in relation to changing demands from other subsystems and from needs of the society as a whole. Engineers, unfortunately, have not had much experience in analyzing even adaptive *technical* systems; that limited art is only now at the conceptual stage. The image of engineering as an adaptive *socio*technical subsystem functioning within the adaptive *socio*technical system of society presents a daunting model to implement. It certainly comes closer to reality, however, than the model of engineering and society as distinct and separate entities. It can at least help inform and orient our thinking.

The aim of the organizing committee from the outset was for a structured set of presentations cumulatively related to the overall theme. We hoped the whole, like the sociotechnical system itself, would be more than the sum of the parts. We were fortunate to engage for the symposium a historian (with an early engineering education), an anthropologist/archaeologist, an economist from industry, and three engineers, one recently in government, one in academia, and one in industrial research. We believe such diversity provides a needed interdisciplinary perspective.

The first two essays relate to the overall sociotechnical system. Thomas Hughes provides a historical and historiographic point of view. As you will see, historians of technology have arrived at the same sociotechnical model to which engineers, I believe, must be driven by logic and their own experience. Robert McC. Adams examines the dynamic interplay between society and its technological subsystem as a complex but unitary relationship in which it is difficult to distinguish with sufficient clarity the intangible but powerful influence of social values either as agencies of change or resistances to change.

The third and fourth essays offer views from the standpoint of two major organizational subsystems of society, business and government. Marina Whitman treats business in terms of the growing tensions and challenges for engineering and engineers in the auto industry as a result of demands for economic growth and jobs and for safer and more environmentally benign automobiles. John Fairclough examines government's desire to ensure economic growth through an orderly and coordinated process of scientific research and the development of a healthy engineering research and development enterprise.

The final two essays offer views of the sociotechnical system by practicing engineers. In doing so, they discuss engineering's response to societal forces in terms of technological delivery systems, and speculate on the core purpose of engineering. George Bugliarello assesses the current social environment for dealing with technological change, as well as expectations of engineering that are frequently at odds with the way engineering is actually taught and practiced.

Robert Lucky offers a model of the sociotechnical system with examples to show that technology in the future will probably continue, as it has in the past, to both lead and follow social change.

We invite you, as you read the essays, to think about them in light of the sociotechnical model put forth above. The essays may not invoke the model explicitly or use the words employed here, but it does, we believe, provide a useful intellectual framework. If you are an engineer, we hope you will be convinced—if you are not already—of the necessity of paying increased attention to the complex social ramifications of what we do. Given the internal demands of our profession, not all engineers can or should function as what one sociologist has called "heterogeneous engineers." To perform engineering's task as a social enterprise, however, the profession as a whole will need to act more consciously in that mode than it has in the past.

Somewhere in his writings, the late, eminent social critic Lewis Mumford said, "The main lesson that history teaches is—prepare for the unexpected." As the Academy proceeds into its second quarter century, we hope this volume of essays will in some small way help our colleagues—as well as the lay public—to make that paradoxical preparation.

WALTER G. VINCENTI
Symposium Chairman

1
Systems Perspectives

From Deterministic Dynamos to Seamless-Web Systems

During the past few decades, the scholarly study of the history of technology has made impressive strides toward placing technological change in a historical perspective and presenting the fruits of historical scholarship in a manner consonant with the experience of engineers, industrial scientists, and managers. Today we see technology as interacting with society; we now study technology as sociotechnical systems. The new history of technology shows that those who wish to preside over technological change need to master social, political, and economic factors as well as technical ones. This new history shows that the engineer's field of action is the sociotechnical system.

One purpose of this essay is to examine progress made in the field of the history of technology and to invite engineers, industrial scientists, and managers to draw on, and contribute to, this available body of knowledge. Another objective is to encourage students in engineering schools to broaden and enrich their understanding of technological change through the study of the new history of technology.

THE SHIFT AWAY FROM INTERNALISM AND DETERMINISM

A quarter century ago, historians of technology were usually presenting earnestly detailed narratives of the development of machines, devices, and processes. Although scholarly and celebratory, the resulting articles and books did not analyze technological change. These histories were positivistic and reductionist in character, virtually ignoring nontechnical and nonscientific factors. Historians of technology now label this mode of presentation and interpretation

7

the internalist approach. It was implicit or explicit in its technological determinism and reductionist in its portrayal of modern technology as primarily applied science and economics.

Technological determinism embodies the widely held belief that hardware and software technology are the ultimate cause of social change. This assumption underlies much that we receive through our news media. We often hear that computers will change our work patterns, that western television will determine attitudes toward capitalism in Eastern Europe, and that nuclear weapons will maintain a lasting peace. Since World War II, it has been forecast that there would be numerous technological revolutions—among them atomic energy, the computer, and the information revolutions—followed by dramatic social changes. Even our scholarly histories still pretend to show how the Industrial Revolution in Britain ushered in modern times. One of the tenets of vulgar Marxism is a dogmatic insistence that technological change brings social change. Only rarely do we read or hear that values or social changes shape technology. When I was in engineering school, I often heard my professors dismiss politics as irrational and irrelevant, and identify technology as the root cause of all social improvement.

A History of Technology, published by Oxford University Press in the mid-1950s, clearly exemplifies the internalist genre in the field of history (Singer et al., 1954–1958). Massively informative, painstakingly organized, and copiously illustrated, the five volumes covering the history until 1990 survey technological and applied science developments chronologically. The editors define technology as "how things are commonly done or made" and "what things are done or made" (Singer et al., 1954, p. vii). Having virtually ignored the social relations of technology, they belatedly conclude their five volumes with an afterthought essay on "technology and its social consequences." In tone the work is internalist and unabashedly technologically deterministic.

The authors contributed chapters defined by engineering and industrial categories. For instance, chapters on electrical technology in the nineteenth century deal with "the generation of electricity" and "the distribution and utilization of electricity." A cataloglike description of the basic discoveries of Alessandro Volta, Hans Christian Oersted, Michael Faraday, and others precede a chronicle describing progressively and more increasingly complex machines and processes, each assigned its basic technical characteristics and associated with the names of preeminent inventors and engineers. Magnetoelectric generators, for instance, give way to self-excited dynamos, and those supplying simple direct current to ones generating polyphase current. Such an approach leads the reader to conclude that technological change is essentially the progressive application of science to solve technical problems, which in turn results in an increasing variety of technical devices and processes of ever-increasing efficiency. Technological development thus takes place in a hermetically sealed world of invention, engineering, and science until the fruit of thought and labor is loosed on the world to have its "social impact." Such history is now termed Whiggish because it, like nineteenth century British liberal gentlemen, presupposed an uncritical belief in progress. One might dismiss this history as well-intentioned and harmless, but this is to overlook the probability that young engineers who are persuaded by the information and interpretation of *A History of Technology* are not likely to consider political and social factors as they design technology or aspire to preside over it.

Another salient characteristic of the internalist approach assumes that modern technology is mostly applied science. This interpretation is congruent with the argument often advanced in the past by science policy advisers that technological application will emerge willy-nilly from our support of pure science. For this reason, internalist history was and is usable history for those seeking support for pure science. History used in this way, however, leads to a misunderstanding of the nature of technological change, and perhaps, in the long run, to ineffective science policy. Today, the new history of technology offers a far more complex interpretation of the relation of science and technology and one far more in accord with the experience of engineers and industrial scientists.

As we have noted, internalist history of technology reinforces disciplinary and industrial category boundaries, taxonomies used often in engineering. For instance, chapters in the *A History of Technology* cover bridges and tunnels, the internal combustion engine, petroleum, machine tools, rubber, and mechanical road transport, to name only a few of the categories. Such organization facilitates the writing of a simple, clear narrative of technical developments but at the same time frustrates the presentation of the interconnections that transcend specialist categories. Using technological categories, for instance, precludes showing the interconnections among the internal combustion engine, petroleum engineering, and mechanical road transport and how such interactions like these helped bring about the modern, or second, industrial revolution. The internalist mode assigns plows to the category of food production and ignores social institutions like the medieval manor, so major sociotechnical changes such as the agricultural revolution of the early Middle Ages are overlooked. Our effort to understand technological change and to convey this understanding to others will continue to be severely handicapped if we employ only the internalist mode with its emphasis on individual artifacts evolving outside functional relationships to other artifacts and to social institutions.

Technology as Systems

When Lynn White, Jr., published his eloquent, erudite, and brilliant analysis of *Medieval Technology and Social Change* in 1962, he provided a new model of historical research and writing. He offered a viable alternative to an essential aspect of the internalist approach and new insights into the nature of technological change. He writes in a determinist mode, but his identification

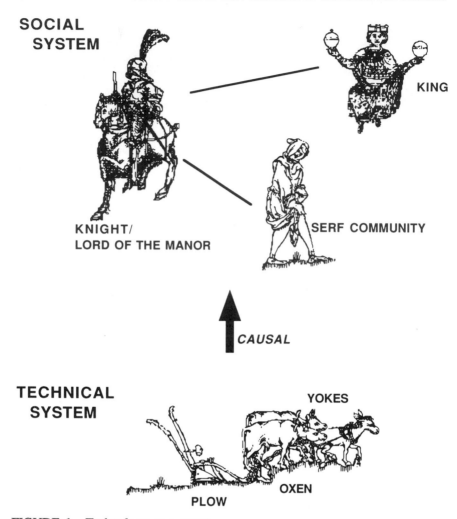

SOCIAL SYSTEM

KING

**KNIGHT/
LORD OF THE MANOR**

SERF COMMUNITY

CAUSAL

TECHNICAL SYSTEM

YOKES

OXEN

PLOW

FIGURE 1   Technology as systems.

of technology as systems rather than as isolated artifacts radically departs from the internalist approach. As a result, his history portrays complex and encompassing social change caused by evolving, interacting technology components such as plows, ox teams, and harnesses (Figure 1).

White argues that during an era when nine-tenths of the population of medieval Europe was involved in tillage, changes in the mode of plowing modified population, wealth, political relationships, leisure, and cultural expression (White, 1962, p. 39) and brought about one of the most prevailing and characteristic social institutions of the Middle Ages, the medieval manor. He also persuasively portrays the introduction of the stirrup as dramatically altering the nature of medieval warfare in Western Europe. "Few inventions," he writes, "have been so simple as the stirrup, but few have had so catalytic an influence on history." This advance ushered in the social system of feudalism dominated by an aristocracy of warriors endowed with land that sustained a new and highly specialized way of fighting. "Antiquity imaged the Centaur; the early Middle Ages made him the master of Europe" (White, 1962, p. 38).

We sample White's approach in more detail in his portrayal of the agricultural revolution of the Middle Ages, where he poses a problem familiar to engineers—that of transferring technology from one material and cultural environment to another. In late Roman and early medieval times, as people moved northward from the Italian peninsula, the peasant left the dry sandy earth and relatively dry climate to encounter the heavy alluvial soil of the river valleys and wet weather of northern Europe. In the south had evolved a technological system involving the scratch-plow with two oxen, shallow cross-plowing in easily pulverized, moisture-retaining solid, and square fields. After encountering the heavy, moisture-laden soil of the north, the tiller of the soil adopted a different system. The interacting components invented and developed included the wheeled heavy plow, with a coulter to cut vertically into the sod; a plowshare to slash the earth horizontally at the grass roots; and a mouldboard to turn the slice of earth to right or left. This heavier plow required eight yoked oxen to pull it. Because no cross-plowing was needed, the fields became long and narrow rather than square. This system substituted efficiently applied animal power for human energy and time and illustrates the sequential substitution of new components in a system of agriculture.[1] Since few peasants owned eight oxen, they had to pool their animals, combine their land holdings into large open fields, and coordinate their planting and plowing. Communal decisions were made by a powerful village council of peasants. Thus did the characteristic manorial economy, a sociotechnical system, emerge.[2]

Engineers, industrial scientists, and managers who preside over technological change today will also find congenial White's presentation of the dynamics of systems evolving. The introduction of the heavy plow, he reasoned, was only the first critical technological event of an extended sequence of innovations during the agricultural revolution of the early Middle Ages. Take for example the gradual substitution of the horse for the ox as draft animal. The introduction of a new harness and a nailed shoe made the horse an economic as well as military asset. A harnessed and shod horse moved so much more rapidly than the ox that, according to modern experiments, "he produces 50 percent more foot-pounds per second" and is also able to work one or two hours longer each day (White, 1962, p. 62). His circle of reasoning closes as he asserts that the new three-field system of crop rotation, stimulated by the introduction of the heavy plow, brought the cultivation of oats for the horse, and legumes for humans. With the cost of horse feed thus made lower than that of ox feed, the horse repeatedly displaced the ox. White summarizes his account of systems evolving and revolutions transpiring as follows:

> It is not merely the new quantity of food produced by improved agricultural methods, but the new type of food supply which goes far towards explaining, for northern Europe at least, the startling expansion of population, the growth and multiplication of cities, the rise in industrial production, the outreach of commerce, and the new exuberance of spirits which enlivened that age. In the full sense of the vernacular, the Middle Ages, from the tenth century onward, were full of beans (White, 1962, p. 76).

Dynamics of Technological Change

In history, as in science and technology, articulating patterns of change helps us see our world in new ways. White showed us systems of technological relationships, and other historians soon after explicitly identified technological systems in the historical events and structures they studied. Relationships and connections that had been previously overlooked in the source materials now emerged as historians pushed in new directions the idea of technology as evolving systems.

When I began writing a biography of Elmer Sperry, the biographical material published about his 1910 invention of the gyrocompass presented it as an isolated event in a series of seemingly unrelated inventive acts spread over his lifetime (Hughes, 1973). Internalist accounts of the invention only described the complex device and noted the substantial contribution made to navigation. If we consider the gyrocompass as a component and the ship as a system, however, then exciting insights into Sperry's invention of the compass follow. Since the mid-nineteenth century, steam engines displaced sails, wooden hulls gave way to iron ones, and electric motors and lights replaced steam-powered and petroleum-illuminated devices. An unintended consequence of the alteration of these components was the effect on other ship components. Changes cascaded through the system. For example, the ship was now filled with magnetic flux from the newly introduced iron hull, and electromagnetic fields generated by its electric motors, which affected the magnetic compass used to guide the wooden ship. Now the magnetic compass responded to these fields in addition to the magnetic field of the earth. Because of the improvement in gunnery and gunpowders, this malfunction became especially troublesome. With longer firing ranges possible, gunfire errors from flawed compass readings were magnified. Sperry and other inventors learned of this reverse salient in the evolving ship system and concentrated their creative talents on the solution of the problem (Figure 2). Research and development funds available because of an intensifying armaments race supported their inventive activities. By the eve of World War I, several inventors, including Sperry, had introduced the gyrocompass, a device unaffected by the irregularities of magnetic fields, but

1850-1880

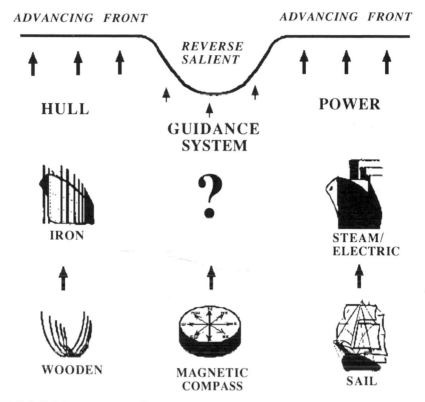

FIGURE 2 Solving reverse salients.

dependent on the rotation of the earth. In this case, the inventors responded to a system undergoing dynamic change.

Based on my research on the development of the gyrocompass as a complex of systematic relationships, I then developed a model of technological systems evolving in which purposeful changes in some components in a technological system often lead to unintended malfunctions in others. Thus, alert inventors who monitor these omnipresent modern technological systems as they expand can then concentrate on inventions that solve the problems of the malfunctioning components. Once the system is in equilibrium, the opportunities for invention disappear, but as long as so-called improvements are being made, the cascading effect keeps inventors, industrial researchers, and others busy.

This Sperry episode, however, presumes too narrow a model of technological systems. Sperry also extended his horizons to encompass a sociotechnical system with nontechnical as well as technical components. Early in his career as an inventor, he found that new technology, including the gyrocompass, was rarely developed by existing institutions. Only infrequently did he locate an established manufacturing firm willing to abandon a line of products in which it had heavily invested skill, knowledge, and capital in order to develop a new innovation unrelated to its investment. So, on numerous occasions he, the inventor-entrepreneur, had to invent not only a device but an institution for manufacturing and marketing as well. Perusing his papers, one realizes that he drew no distinctions among the technical, the economic, and the institutional. The proposition that creativity is holistic can be grounded in empirical evidence. As he invented, Sperry wove a seamless web of technology and institutional change.

Involving the Visible Hand

It was Alfred D. Chandler who further enlarged our historical horizons with his Pulitzer prize-winning volume, *The Visible Hand* (1977), in which he stresses the interaction of technology and institutions, especially the means of production and the business corporations that managed these. Not unlike White, Chandler tends to technological determinism. He argues that modern management practices make it possible for us to enter the doors that technology opens. He is especially adept at showing how modern management used the infrastructure of communication and transportation to coordinate and control the interacting means of production and distribution. Using examples from the period of about 1850 to 1950, when the market for goods in the United States was expanding, Chandler shows how the visible hand of management ensures the smooth flow of materials and energy through the stages of production and distribution, which continuously evolve because of technological innovation.

From Chandler, we learn to understand technological change better if we take into consideration the role of the manager and the firm. White's insistence that the multioxen team and deep plow brought about the institution of the manor, which in turn presided over the new technology, finds a counterpart in Chandler's argument that modern large-scale, capital-intensive technology paves the way for the multidivisional corporation which then rationalizes production through management. Chandler demonstrates that the implications of the technology revolution that transpired from about 1880 to 1930—the Second Industrial Revolution—would not have been realized without managerial, or organizational, innovations. In other words, the introduction of modern multidivisional business corporations contributed as much to increased production and productivity during the Second Industrial Revolution as did, say, the electric power system. Historians of technology attempting to explain the Second

Industrial Revolution now realize that, in addition to lectures on machine tools, steel production, and petroleum refining, they must include the rise of modern scientific management among their lecture topics.

In his new book, *Scale and Scope*, Chandler gives an example of how modern corporations realize the implications of technological change. After 1882, in order to maximize the flow of materials from well to consumer, managers of the Standard Oil Trust integrated new modes of petroleum refining and highly developed means of transportation and communication. Muckraking historians have characterized the formation of such trusts as efforts to establish profit-gouging enterprises. Chandler, by contrast, explains how the Standard Oil Trust provided a legal instrument to exploit the potential of modern technology. The management of the trust, through stock interchanges and other financial devices, controlled a loose federation of 40 companies, which owned oil fields, refineries, and transportation networks. Afterward, rationalization concentrated about a quarter of the world's kerosene production into three large and technically efficient refineries. As a result, economies of scale drastically lowered the cost of producing kerosene (Chandler, 1990, p. 24–25). Chandlerian managers fulfilled the goal that Thorstein Veblen defined early in this century when he called for production engineers to transform the nation's industry into "a system of interlocking mechanical processes" (Veblen, 1921, pp. 72–74).

Geographical Determinism

Although more sophisticated and subtle in their interpretations of technological change than the internalists, White and Chandler are, as we have noted, technological determinists. It was left to other historians to successfully attack the citadel of technological determinism and provide fresh understanding of the nature of technological change. Several decades before White and Chandler, Louis Hunter, an American economic historian, wrote vividly and concretely about the way in which geographic forces shape technology. Considering the persuasiveness of Hunter's monograph, one is surprised that internalist, technological-determinist history continued to prevail. Perhaps this is because Hunter was an economic historian, considered outside the mainstream of the historians of technology in his time.

Hunter's seminal work bears the memorable title *Steamboats on the Western Rivers* (1949). It is a marvelous example of comparative history on why steamboats navigating eastern coastal waters and rivers differed in technical detail from those on the Mississippi and it tributaries. After reading Hunter, it is difficult to argue that there is one best way to do technology, regardless of place. Hunter takes an ecological approach by placing technology in a geographic setting and showing how the technical characteristics mirror geographical features.

Robert Fulton, a steamboat inventor, made the mistake of assuming that technology could be transferred from one geographical region to another without substantial modification. After successfully introducing steamboat transportation along the Hudson river, he obtained a monopoly to provide steamboat transportation along the Mississippi. He persuaded Nicholas Roosevelt, a New Jersey steam-engine builder, and workmen from New York to set up a factory in Pittsburgh to build steamboats much like those used on the Hudson and eastern coastal waters. The engines were efficient, low-pressure, and condensing, and the hulls were long and narrow, sitting deep in the water.

Within a few years, however, by 1818, Fulton abandoned his monopoly because his type of steamboat was superseded by broad-beamed, shallow-draft vessels with relatively inefficient, noncondensing, high-pressure steam engines. This new design, of indigenous origin, resulted from the empirical instincts and craft skills of engine designers and shipbuilders familiar with the geography of the Mississippi and its tributaries (Figure 3). Their high-pressure engine without condenser and air pump was lighter than the condensing engine, so their vessel rode higher in the shallows of the Mississippi, which was plagued with sandbars and snags. Their high-pressure engine offered more reserve power to negotiate extreme variations of current and depth; the noncondensing engine was not befouled by the muddy western waters; the less efficient engine used low-cost wood fuel in the still unsettled Mississippi Valley; and the broad-beamed hull had less draft than the eastern boats customarily used on the bays and tributary rivers. From Hunter's monograph historians and students learn about the realities of technology transfer and the absurdity of arguing that there is one best engineering solution.

POLITICAL FACTORS

Hunter shows us that the concept of technological determinism alone fails to encompass the complexity of technological change. He demonstrates that geography often shapes or determines the development of technology. Other historians have recently shown how factors other than geography can also shape technology. If we consider the history of the comparative developments of electric light and power systems in the United States, Great Britain, and Germany early in this century, we find technological determinism once again flawed. In this case political factors shaped the technology. The story begins by comparing the backward electric supply system of London with that of Chicago. The Chicago supply had been consolidated into a single system with a high load factor and low cost, supplied by several large turbine-driven power stations, while greater London had 65 electrical utilities, 70 generating stations averaging a little over 5,000 kilowatts in capacity, and 49 different types of supply systems, 10 different frequencies, 32 voltage levels for transmission and 24 for distribution. A Londoner might toast bread in the morning, light the office during dark days, walk home under street lights, and read by lamps at

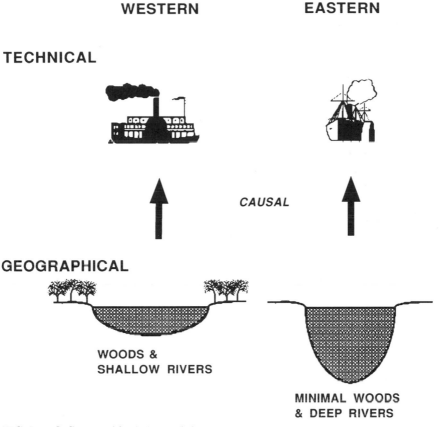

FIGURE 3 Geographical determinism.

home—all with different kinds of electricity. The overall load factor was low, costs were high, and usage was small by comparison with other metropolitan centers, especially those in the United States and Germany (Hughes, 1983, p. 227). Such was the British electrical industry lag, a cause for concern in an era when electric supply was a symbol of progress and power, political as well as technological.

An internalist historian would seek the cause of Britain's technological malaise in generators, motors, transformers, and engineers less efficient and science less well developed than those in Germany or the United States. Resort to the original sources does not sustain such a thesis. British science, especially physics, enjoyed great prestige, with achievement to match; the red brick universities offered electrical engineering courses comparable in content to those in the United States and Germany, and the many and varied power stations were small but recognized as exceedingly well designed by painstaking engineers who used electrical equipment manufactured not only in Britain, but imported from, or designed in, the United States as well as Germany. The question of the lag could only baffle the internalist.

If, however, the historian looks beyond the confines of the world of technical and scientific affairs, beyond the reach of the internalist and the determinist, clues about the causes of the British electrical industry lag can be found. Original sources reveal that experienced British engineers and managers did look beyond the dynamos, transformers, and motors, all the way to the Houses of Parliament, where since 1882 a series of legislative enactments regulating electrical supply had emerged. About this legislation the engineers of the venerable Institution of Electrical Engineers declared

> We hold that electrical enterprises should have their limits and boundaries set by economical considerations only, and that arbitrary boundaries, mostly of medieval ecclesiastical origin, should not limit the distribution or the growth of electrical systems (Hughes, 1983, pp. 233–234).

This text expressed the fundamental modern tension between a technocratic vision and a political ideology. The boundaries of medieval origin are those of the traditional local governments in Britain, the vestries, parishes, and counties. The British had long cherished these institutions and they realized that if technological systems, such as the electrical, transcended them geographically, they would likewise transcend their local authority. Local governments could not regulate or acquire electric light and power systems that spread over and beyond their political jurisdiction. Transformers in one authority and power plants in another would frustrate regulation then and now.

This episode provides a striking revelation of legislation shaping technology. One can probe even deeper and observe political power and values shaping the legislation and the technology. Those 75 power stations in London clearly state the message: "we are modern artifacts but we are shaped by values originating in medieval England." This is not technological determinism; this is value construction of technology. In this instance, technology-shaping values were institutionalized into the legislation.

SOCIAL CONSTRUCTION OF TECHNOLOGY

By 1980, historians of technology had abandoned the deterministic simplicities of the internalist approach. Technological systems for many had become the unit of study, and many saw geographical and political, as well as economic, factors as shaping technology. Some sociologists interested in technology were soon insisting that social factors must be there as well. In 1984, historians of like mind joined the sociologists at a conference in the Netherlands and articulated the social construction approach. From this conference emerged a volume of papers providing generalized argument and case histories. It was appropriately titled, *The Social Construction of Technological Systems* (Bijker et al., 1987). In their essays, the authors identified professional status, education and practical experience, economic and institutional interests, and values among those social forces shaping technology.

In essence, social construction holds that technological systems bear the imprint of the social context in which they arise (Pfaffenberger, 1990, p. 15). Because many design alternatives exist, social interests, as well as other nontechnical factors, can play key roles in shaping the artifacts produced or the style of a system constructed from these artifacts. Pinch and Bijker (1987, pp. 17–50) show that during the late nineteenth century, different social groups such as sports cyclists, tourist cyclists, elderly men, and woman cyclists posed different sets of problems to which different producers responded with various solutions called bicycles. It was not at all clear to contemporaries which variants would "die" and which would "survive." The power and strength of the various social groups contending to define a bicycle ultimately determined its technical characteristics, including the meaning attached to it. There was no one best solution, but a number of solutions, the surviving one or ones emerging from the context of social interest groups. Few would dispute the argument presented by Pinch and Bijker, but how many of us see, as they do, technology as congealed social interests?

We find another example of the social construction of technology in the history of the development of a cooling system for atomic reactors built during World War II. From the early days of the Manhattan Project, engineers and scientists differed about the best method of cooling plutonium-generating reactors. Some advocated gas and others liquid cooling. There was also disagreement over which gas and which liquid. One might analyze the episode in an internalist way and simply suggest that the search continued until the one best solution was found. Reflection and a social constructivist mode of interpretation result instead in a more complex and realistic analysis. The "best way" for engineers turned out to be different from the "best way" for scientists. Generally the engineers, especially those of the DuPont Company, following the dictates of experience, conservatively opted for gaseous cooling, either helium or air. Physicist Leo Szilard wanted to use the exotic coolant liquid bismuth. (With Albert Einstein he had patented in the 1930s a refrigerator using a liquid metal as a coolant.) Drawing on theoretical analysis, Eugene Wigner, also a physicist, recommended water cooling, the mode eventually adopted (Hughes, 1990, pp. 391–394). Professional background and experience clearly shaped the positions taken. There are a number of cases in the early history of nuclear energy showing how engineers differed from physicists on the best solution for technical problems.

Donald MacKenzie (1987) offers a variation of the social construction approach that introduces interaction between technology and social context. MacKenzie shows how interest groups with different technical capabilities and strategic and tactical objectives influenced the accuracy of missile guidance systems and how, in turn, the development of missile accuracy shaped strategic and tactical objectives. "Technological developments," he argues, "cannot be treated in isolation from organizational, political, and economic matters." This argument is not a contribution to the old debate on the social responsibility of the engineer: it contributes to our understanding of the nature of engineering design and technological change. From his interviews with engineers in the missile guidance field MacKenzie concludes that there is a rough correlation between how articulate they are on issues involving interactions of technical and nontechnical factors, and their worldly success.

He shows how successful system builders such as Charles Stark Draper engineered technical, economic, and political matters simultaneously. The drive of Draper and his laboratory for maximum missile accuracy was determined not only by technical considerations, but by the choice of problems that they, with their particular interests and capabilities, could solve. They believed that the historical experiences of their laboratory had given it a bias toward solving problems of accuracy at the expense at times of other problems such as reliability and cost. Other laboratories and manufacturers working in concert with government agencies decided on missile guidance technology that emphasized reliability and cost (MacKenzie, 1987, pp. 195–222). Clearly there was more than one best solution, a view rarely encountered in journalistic discussions of technology or in the curricula of our engineering schools.

TECHNOLOGY-SCIENCE RELATIONSHIP

As we have noted, the internalist approach to technology was wedded not only to technological determinism but also to the proposition that technology is applied science. This internalist persuasion was reinforced after World War II by influential technology policymakers, such as Vannevar Bush, a wartime mobilizer of science and technology and postwar author of *Endless Horizons* (1946), who wrote:

> Basic research leads to new knowledge. It provides scientific capital. It creates the fund from which the practical applications of knowledge must be drawn. New products and new processes do not appear full-grown. They are founded on new principles and new conceptions, which in turn are painstakingly developed by research in the purest realms of science (Bush, 1946, pp. 52–53).

No clearer argument that technology is applied science could be made. This view was echoed repeatedly both by those seeking funding for pure science and those seeking status for engineering by associating it with prestigious postwar physics.

Research by historians, however, did not support the Bush proposition. In still-frequently cited articles written in the early 1970s, Edwin T. Layton, Jr.,

FIGURE 4 Science of technology.

counters both Bush's argument and the similar one found in the internalist *A History of Technology*. Layton believes that knowledge generated by science is not sufficient for engineers involved in designing artifacts and technological systems (Figure 4). "Science may indeed influence technology. . . . But this does not provide an adequate explanation of most technological change" (Layton, 1974, p. 39). Technology, he maintains, is an independent system of thought different from—and derived from sources not limited to—science. He refers to the mirror-image characteristics of the technological and scientific communities. The differences inhere in the ends of the two communities, for scientists seek to know, and technologists seek to design means to fulfill societal ends (Layton, 1971, pp. 576–578).[3]

In a series of four articles in *Technology and Culture*, Walter Vincenti, an aeronautical engineer and historian, also provides a thoughtful and informative reading of the technology-science relationship. Simple concepts of technology as applied science did not survive his scrutiny. He explores in depth various aspects of engineering knowledge in the contexts of experimental research, theoretical analysis, and production and design. He is especially interested in discovering whether or not peculiarly technological methodologies exist. To formulate and test his hypotheses, he examines several case histories, including the air-propeller tests of W. F. Durand and E. P. Lesley, the development of control-volume analysis from 1910 to 1925, the innovation of flush riveting in American airplanes, and the problem of airfoil design in connection with the Davis wing (Vincenti 1979; 1982; 1984; 1986).

Vincenti's studies lead him to conclude that technological methods of experimentation differ both in form and object from those in the physical sciences. Technological methods permit the engineer to obtain information needed for design when no usable theoretical knowledge is available. Vincenti also finds that an engineering science exists and that it differs from other science in that the engineering science is acquired in order to serve the needs of engineers who design artifacts such as fluid flow devices. Moreover, in the case of airfoil technology, Vincenti decides that over a period of years design engineers moved from a methodology that was essentially cut-and-try to one laden with theory derived from the cumulative experience of design and use. As a result, they were able to greatly reduce uncertainty. These and his other conclusions leave no doubt that engineering science and experimentation have developed alongside methodologies in natural sciences. From Vincenti we have more evidence that Vannevar Bush and others were far off the mark when they insisted that engineering, or technology, was essentially the application of natural science.

CONCLUSION

Over the past few decades the historian's understanding of the nature of technological change has developed dramatically. Today most historians of technology consider a descriptive narrative that ignores the interacting technical, economic, political, and social components of technological change reductionist and distorting. New modes of research and presentation take the technological, or the sociotechnical, system rather than individual artifacts as the unit of study. Deterministic dynamos have given way to seamless-web systems.

In my writing on the history of electrical technology, I present it as an evolving system of interaction among such components as turbines, dynamos, high-voltage grids, electrical utility management structure, electrical engineering departments in engineering schools, investment banks, regulatory agencies, and the weight of public opinion (Figure 5). Presiding over sociotechnical systems are system builders, including inventors, engineers, managers, and financiers who have prevailed during successive stages of system growth.

Epistemological developments of the magnitude of those taking place in the study of the history of technology during recent decades would surely be considered highly significant in a field of engineering or science. I suggest that engineers and scientists consider the impact that the new history of technology should have on their understanding of technological change.

The understanding derived from the new history can be used to encourage engineers and industrial scientists to present a more complex and less reductionist view when they explain technological change to laymen and policymakers. A reductionist view often leads to the application of unworkable technical fixes for problems that are in essence complex, multifaceted systems. Furthermore, the presentation of this more complex view of change will help laymen and policymakers appreciate that technological change, like political change, is complicated and deserves the attention of our most capable and imaginative leaders.

This new understanding can also be used to reform engineering and science education. At this time and for decades past, U.S. engineering and science

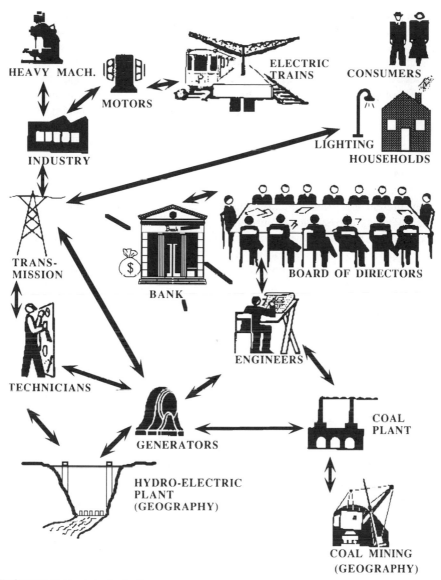

FIGURE 5 Sociotechnical system.

schools have left the impression with their graduates—in part due to the intellectual ambience of the engineering school that inculcates an unreflective technological determinism—that technological change results simply from the solution of technical and scientific problems. Students leave school with the mistaken impression that political and social factors are extraneous. If the arguments offered in this essay are valid, then these young professionals are being ill-prepared to preside over either technological change or the development of sociotechnical systems. Experience may in time relieve them of this indoctrination, but why the prolongation of innocence in engineering education? Those of us who teach history to those who will become lawyers, businessmen, politicians, and other makers of the modern world do not dare shield them from the realities of change.

Courses introducing the complex realities of technological change should not be relegated to elective status for professionally oriented students. Doing so implies that the social and political components of change are peripheral. As I have shown in this essay, the political or social components and the problems they present are often the core constituent of the problem complex to which the engineers and scientists must address themselves. I can provide countless examples of experienced engineers and scientists who focused their energies on political and social matters in order to bring about innovation. If we do not prepare engineers and scientists for this imaginative flexibility, then we must relegate responsibility for long-range technological change to other professions.

NOTES

1. White notes that historians and archaeologists have many exceptions to the rule that the heavy plow brought a system of cultivation, but he believes that this was the typical development.
2. This follows White's argument as he presents it in *Medieval Technology and Social Change*, pp. 39–57.
3. For an informed and thoughtful essay on the science-technology relationship, see John M. Staudenmaier (1985, pp. 83–120).

REFERENCES

Bijker, W., T. Hughes, T. Pinch, eds. 1987. The Social Construction of Technological Systems: New Directions in the Sociology and History of Technology. Cambridge, Mass.: MIT Press.

Bush, V. 1946. Endless Horizons. Washington, D.C.: Public Affairs Press. Reprint, 1975. New York: Arno Press.

Chandler, A. 1990. Scale & Scope: The Dynamics of Industrial Capitalism. Boston: Harvard University Press.

Chandler, A. 1977. The Visible Hand: The Managerial Revolution in American Business. Cambridge, Mass.: Belknap Press.

Hughes, T. 1973. Elmer Sperry: Inventor and Engineering. Baltimore: Johns Hopkins University Press.

Hughes, T. 1983. Networks of Power: Electrification in Western Society, 1880–1930. Baltimore: Johns Hopkins University Press.

Hughes, T. 1990. American Genesis: A Century of Invention and Technological Enthusiasm, 1870–1970. New York: Penguin.

Hunter, L. 1949. Steamboats on the Western Rivers, An Economic and Technological History. Cambridge, Mass.: Harvard University Press.

Layton, E. 1971. Mirror-image twins: The communities of science and technology in 19th century America. Technology and Culture 12:562–80.

Layton, E., 1974. Technology as knowledge. Technology and Culture 15:31–41.

MacKenzie, D. 1987. Missile accuracy: A case study in the social processes of technological change. Pp. 195–222 in The Social Construction of Technological Systems: New Directions in the Sociology and History of Technology, W. Bijker, T. Hughes, and T. Pinch, eds. 1987. Cambridge, Mass.: MIT Press.

Pfaffenberger, B. 1990. Democratizing Information: Online Databases and the Rise of End-user Searching. Boston: G. K. Hall & Company.

Pinch, T., and W. Bijker. 1987. The social construction of facts and artifacts: Or how the sociology of science and the sociology of technology might benefit each other. Pp. 17–50 in The Social Construction of Technological Systems: New Directions in the Sociology and History of Technology, W. Bijker, T. Hughes, and T. Pinch, eds. 1987. Cambridge, Mass.: MIT Press.

Singer, C., E. J. Holmyard, A. Hall, and T. Williams, eds. 1954–58. A History of Technology. New York: Oxford University Press.

Staudenmaier, J. M. 1985. Technology's Storytellers: Reweaving the Human Fabric. Cambridge, Mass.: MIT Press.

Veblen, T. 1921. The Engineers and the Price System. Second Edition 1963. New York: Harcourt, Brace and World.

Vincenti, W. 1979. The air-propeller tests of W. F. Durand and E. P. Lesley: A case study in technology methodology. Technology and Culture 20:712–751.

Vincenti, W. 1982. Control-volume analysis: A difference in thinking between engineering and physics. Technology and Culture 23:145–174.

Vincenti, W. 1984. Technological knowledge without science: The innovation of flush riveting in American airplanes, ca. 1930–ca. 1950. Technology and Culture 25:540–576.

Vincenti, W. 1986. The Davis wing and the problem of airfoil design: Uncertainty and growth in engineering knowledge. Technology and Culture 27:717–758.

White, L., Jr. 1962. Medieval Technology and Social Change. Oxford: Clarendon Press.

Cultural and Sociotechnical Values

ROBERT McC. ADAMS

Values surely play a part, and sometimes perhaps an important one, in the loosely articulated bundle of subsystems composing human society. But to what extent and under what circumstances does that part ever become determinative? Can we, more particularly, identify and isolate some of the major impacts that values have on whatever set of other subsystems contains (most of) engineering? The reflections on these questions given here are frankly those of a skeptic, doubtful that cultural values constitute a superior, autonomous domain with which more mundane activities like technology must somehow be brought into harmony.

This agnosticism admittedly may be idiosyncratic, a result of my involvement for many years with prevailingly impersonal themes of demography, economy, and ecology across millennial spans of early Near Eastern history. In that setting it was seldom possible to distinguish values with sufficient clarity to credit them with a significant role either as agencies of change or resistance to change. But more recently, and now in a more commonplace role as an administrator and policy-oriented social scientist, I continue to find values themselves intangible and evanescent while readily conceding that values are in the air we breathe and surely influence in some way much of what we think and do.

On the other hand, each successive action we take, individually or in association, subtly changes the mosaic of standards by which we assess our own behavior or that of others. Granting that those mosaics simultaneously constrain and influence our perceptions and actions, how could they not also be continually tested and redefined by the circumstances we encounter or bring about? In short, I believe it is fundamentally mistaken to elevate values to a

26

permanence and status above the reach of reappraisal or controversy. Doing so diminishes rather than explains their significance.

As values are dynamic and situationally evolving, so they both rationalize and are at the same time continuously shaped by the courses of action we choose. Of course, this must be no less true of engineering than of any other profession, even if at first glance it may seem to be reactive and rooted in a more elemental attempt to cope with material exigencies rather than active and value-driven. After all, few definitions of engineering or technology are free of moral overtones, as exemplified by the suggestion that their "basic function is the expansion of the realm of practical human possibility" (Brooks, 1980, p. 65).

So it is my own view that advancing technology is at once a value position to whose defense engineers (and others) can and should justifiably rise as protagonists, and at the same time a vast program of practical, day-to-day activity carried out in the same spirit. And to maintain its effectiveness, engineering must systematically extend itself beyond its familiar concern for the modification of nature. Borrowing a felicitous phrase from Herbert Simon (1981), engineering encompasses most of the sciences of the artificial, and social engineering is inexpungibly among them. Simple efficacy in a complex, socially ordered world demands modes of application that are sociotechnical rather than narrowly technical.

This leads, however, to the obvious further point that we live in a world of contending value positions that coexist uneasily but completely supersede or displace one another only rarely. It is undeniable that substantial segments of the electorate in most industrialized societies view with increasing indifference or hostility at least some fruits of technology—products and processes that engineers have taken pride in creating and probably regard as unambiguously life-enhancing. Contradictory perceptions always tend to be selectively fixated on hardware; conflicts demand and generate their own inanimate symbols. But the real issues are, on closer inspection, almost always both sociotechnical and value-laden. This means that such issues are also highly complex, not easily bounded, and almost never neatly terminated. Considerations of efficacy once again require that we recognize the multiple, interactive levels at which they engage everyone's attention and are actuated in their practices.

As this suggests, it is a dangerous oversimplification to dismiss most issues of angry partisanship for or against some particular technology as ritualized collisions over irreconcilable values, immune to new information or the give-and take of rational argument. Fundamental clashes of value may indeed sometimes occur, and then often attain a momentum of their own and continue indefinitely. But on closer inspection, it generally turns out that neither side is the undiluted locus of truth, wisdom, or social equity. The right degrees and institutional affiliations make it easy to claim the cloak of specialized authority, but much of the public rightly recognizes—even when seemingly preoccupied with absolutist values—that the cloak of technical expertise often slips.

RISK, UNCERTAINTY, AND PUBLIC TRUST

The rapidly growing field of contention over technical assessments of risk and uncertainty provides a case in point. Technical assessments abound on risks to health, for example, but so do legal, legislative, and regulatory challenges to them that frequently commission their own, conflicting technical assessments. Adversarial proceedings over the reputed toxic or carcinogenic effects of substances like agent orange, alar, asbestos, chlorofluorocarbons, fluoridated water, polychlorinated biphenyls, and tetraethyl lead (merely to sample a long list) no doubt reflect a high level of public concern. Given the poignancy and vividness of that concern, it not surprisingly then captures a large and growing share of the domestic attention of our media.

It is inevitable that values play a considerable part in these exercises, for they are concerned with prospects of suffering, the blind capriciousness and hence seeming unfairness of the random blow, and the finality of death. Yet despite the depth and even terror of the issues involved, too many of the technical experts who deal with risk address only matters of statistical precision and remain remote from the real issues of distributive justice: Risk for whom, chosen from among what range of alternatives, and with what range of alternative modes of recompense? How speculative or subjective, and how candidly admitted, are the measures of uncertainty that tend to be applied to highly improbable events? What can be done to provide assurance to rising public doubts that all "reasonable" second- and third-order consequences of new technological modifications of the existing or natural order have been anticipated, as examples accumulate in which this plainly turns out not to be the case?

Those who would address risk as a primarily technical and statistical problem have failed to notice that these increasingly salient issues of distributive justice can independently affect public perceptions of risk, and that variations in the latter can produce second-order effects that sometimes far outstrip statistically based computations of cost or frequency. As one noted student of the subject has recently observed,

> In becoming a central cultural construct in America, the word [risk] has changed its meaning. It has entered politics and in so doing has weakened its old connection with technical calculations of probability. . . . The word has been preempted to mean bad risks. The promise of good things in contemporary political discourse is couched in other terms. The language of risk is reserved as a specialized lexical register for political talk about undesirable outcomes. Risk is invoked for a modern-style riposte against abuse of power (Douglas, 1990, pp. 2–3).

Fueling public distrust is what thus turns out to be the self-fulfilling but accurate perception that risk consequences are frequently far graver and more disruptive than advance calculations indicate. The public is aware, and engineers cannot afford to be less sensitive to this, that prominently mentioned, conveniently estimable, direct consequences of unanticipated scientific or technological failures seldom cover the full range, cost, and persistence of subsequent effects. Second-order consequences may include (to mention only a few of them): insurance rate increases; declining property values; economic disruptions resulting from a cessation of tourism, or from shifts in consumer demand for products believed—whether accurately or not—to be somehow associated with other products found faulty or dangerous; and, as was shown at Three Mile Island, persistent effects even on the mental health of the adjacent population. It is simply unrealistic for those advocating new or improved technologies to dismiss such costs from consideration as if they were externalities unrelated to technological risk.

There is also a valid public perception that technological risk probabilities frequently have been grossly underestimated. From a narrowly technological viewpoint, for example, "driver error, pilot error, and human error," are often dismissed as outside the frame of calculation because they arise from human fallibility rather than machine malfunction. But the human controller and the machine together constitute a single system in their operation, and certainly affect the public precisely as if they were a single system. The machine and its operative need to be incorporated in designs as if they constituted a common, closely interacting set of capabilities and weaknesses.

Tragic outcomes of obscure, highly improbable risks have, of course, a special attraction for the media, but it is nevertheless hard to escape the impression that far too little time and effort is currently being devoted to analyzing the tails of probability curves. Performance will always fall short in certain instances, but without greater and more systematic attention, the number of egregious errors threatens to pass a threshold that will inspire general public disbelief in the process of estimation itself. While conflict of interest is always a possibility to be guarded against, the prevailing sources of error are less direct but no less damaging. A common one is unforeseen interactions of system components, under what may be an almost indefinitely wide array of different permutations and combinations of component (including human component) failure. As systems themselves become more complex, this problem can only increase in frequency and severity.

Particularly to be guarded against, it seems to me, is the understandable tendency to stake out the terrain of risk analysis within the disciplinary limits of those performing it. We should not be surprised if the greatest dangers then emerge along the neglected margins and interstices of those fields. Who assumes responsibility for maintaining an enveloping, continuous perspective rather than merely a specialized one? Are engineers satisfied to defer to technically ill-equipped generalists in this crucial respect?

An excellent example of the tendency to work within a narrow disciplinary focus, and its attendant dangers, has been developed by Victoria Tschinkel (1989). Physicians, she points out, were the first to turn their attention to the effects of human activities on the water supply. Through their efforts, the spread of cholera was much reduced by removing sewage from populated areas. Raw sewage added to water bodies that were also the sources of drinking water led, however, to a new generation of threats to public health. These were met, on the advice of a different set of specialists, by chlorination and the consequent, virtual elimination of typhoid. But now, once again, we find we have been left with a system that admirably met its earlier design criteria but failed to keep in view the whole problem. Besides wasting tremendous quantities of water and nutrients, it bypasses expensive treatment facilities with uncontrolled storm drains, fails almost completely to check discharges of heavy metals and exotic chemicals, and has led to spreading eutrophication and contamination of our increasingly precious wetlands and natural water bodies (Tschinkel, 1989, pp. 159–161).

Of importance comparable to the narrowness of focus this illustrates are other "expert" shortcomings. Insufficient attention is frequently paid, for example, to the fragility of assumptions employed. Also common are expressions of assurance that are incommensurate with available sample sizes, or that fail to take account of low-probability eventualities rather than admit the uncomfortably large element of conjecture they require.

As suggested earlier, risk is an area in which public perceptions often are widely discrepant from quantitatively well-established measurements of past experience. Studies of expressed preference lend support, in particular, to the view that "people are willing to tolerate higher risks from activities seen as highly beneficial" and that "other (perceived) characteristics such as familiarity, control, catastrophic potential, equity, and level of knowledge also seem to influence the relation between perceived risk, perceived benefit, and risk acceptance" (Slovic, 1987, p. 283).

One recent study of the risk perceptions based on a modest sample of respondents suggests that "those who rate their self-knowledge of technologies highly also tend to perceive greater average benefits associated with technologies than those who are less confident about their knowledge" (Wildavsky and Dake, 1990, p. 48). That carefully qualified statement leaves open two alternatives— either that greater knowledge produces greater confidence, or that professedly greater knowledge is a dependent manifestation of greater confidence in the processes and institutions currently producing most technological assessments. Both alternatives are consistent with the significant correlation this study found with a continuum from what it terms a "political culture of hierarchy" to one of "egalitarianism," roughly equated with a continuum from conservatism to liberalism (Wildavsky and Dake, 1990, pp. 49–51).

My own suspicion is that on further study, matters will turn out to be more complex and less easily reduced to ideal-typical contrasts. Conservatism, for example, is as easily associated with individual autonomy and reliance on individual initiative as with a respect for hierarchy. Autonomy no doubt appears in different clusterings of associated attitudes, but it has undeniably become a pervasive value:

> We live in a culture that prizes autonomy. Against that background, our responses to risk acquire their meanings. We respond differently to risks that we choose for ourselves and over which we believe we have some degree of control than we do to risks that we do not choose or believe we control. . . .
>
> In light of our commitment to autonomy, it is not unreasonable to think that consent plays a role in the legitimation of risky activity. Its role is important in our political process, which relies on the participation of the governed for legitimacy, and in the marketplace, where the ideal transaction is represented as one of *voluntary* exchange (Teuber, 1990, p. 237).

However, these issues of public concern for equity versus public trust in institutions by no means exhaust the discrepancies between popular perceptions and statistically based calculations of technological risk. Grossly optimistic biases as to the consequences of personal exposure to risk are common. People are more concerned to avoid negative consequences than to secure positive ones of equal likelihood. Treatment of very improbable events tends to be capricious and undependable, sometimes dismissing them entirely and at other times elevating them to a supreme and undebatable level of importance. Nuclear weapons and nuclear power are of course representative of this latter category, but so are such other risks as those exemplified by new chemical technologies whose toxic side-effects are not immediately apparent. The complete elimination of a lesser hazard typically is overvalued, in comparison with a more significant but merely partial reduction of a far greater one. Although the gulf between scientific findings and popular perceptions like these is also frequently exaggerated (Freudenburg, 1988), the more important point is that widely and firmly held public attitudes are no less a part of the real world, needing to be squarely and yet sensitively dealt with, even if they sometimes may seem to border on the irrational.

Let me briefly illustrate complications of this kind. As seen in the far greater preoccupation with the demonstrably small likelihood of nuclear power disasters than with the substantial, known morbidity and mortality resulting from coal-fired generating plants (and mining the coal they consume), the public reacts more strongly to disasters that can be sharply highlighted than to more diffuse conditions of risk. Along the same lines, the carnage on our highways is passively accepted as "accidents," with the imputation of a random mass of personal bad luck or misjudgment, while rare lapses in relatively much safer air transportation provoke exhaustive investigations and expensive countermeasures. Many such cases of an apparent skewing of public perceptions, with profound implications for governmental or corporate policy, may well be to some extent reflections of the operation of underlying cultural values. But it would be no more correct to exclude them from further, open discussion for that reason than it would be to dismiss them as mere psychological aberrations undeserving of engineering attention.

Recognizing that pervasive misunderstandings like these can complicate communications with the public, there is no reason to question the public's reception of new technological innovations that are imposed by governmental action with growing prudence if not suspicion. For engineers venturing out into domains of sociotechnical contention with renewed courage, this means that the public's trust must be sought and earned. Indeed, it was once won over many decades, in a broad tide of technological advances whose sociotechnical consequences visibly promoted the public welfare. More recently the public's trust has been somewhat eroded, although by no means irretrievably lost, in the same gradualistic way.

But to arrest this erosion we must recognize that we are all the losers when technical specialists rely, without acknowledgment, on inadequate, error-laden analytical methodologies. My own service as a reviewer of many National Research Council studies has painfully familiarized me, for example, with the racking internal arguments, seldom reaching the public, over the questionable simplifications and quantitative precision of many cost-benefit analyses. Closer to a domain where values may indeed play the dominant role, what basis do we ever have for assigning a rate of future discount that establishes the ratio of preference for present returns over the possible welfare of future generations? And that question, of course, brings us face to face with current controversies over whether, how, and how soon to check or demand compensation for the depletion of scarce, publicly owned natural resources or fragile environmental quality.

Builders and protagonists of sociotechnical systems who encounter the public over issues of risk and uncertainty thus enter an arena where values undoubtedly play a significant role. But I have sought to show that values are no more than one of many inputs into the fluid, heavily politicized processes of interaction that account for public responses. To treat them as basic and irreducible is to homogenize the opposition to technological innovation, and thus unwisely to polarize and perhaps paralyze the process.

More hesitantly, I should now like to take up a second set of encounters over sociotechnical issues that seems to support the same general finding. Characterizing it very simplistically, it has to do with public understanding of, let alone confidence in, the reductionist or linear models of explanation that have become our models of discourse since they serve as the standard in science and engineering education.

Perhaps I can best introduce this theme with an admittedly simplistic binary opposition. Karl Popper, the great philosopher of science, is said to have noted once that people can be divided between those who see the world as analogous to clocks, in which cause and effect are always mechanically related, and those who see the world as clouds, each particle acting erratically with only the broad shape of things moving in understandable ways (Sills, 1984). Gross categories like these, to be sure, are never fully applicable to anyone; at best they refer to two arbitrarily distant positions in a continuous distribution. Nevertheless, I think they call attention to another source of friction or misunderstanding that may unnecessarily lead to collisions over supposedly different value positions.

Fundamental changes that to most people are disturbing and unsettling are under way in the structure of our social and economic life. Vast webs of long-distance but narrowly focused interactions erode the integrity of primary social units and substitute for a stable sense of place as an ordering principle in our lives. Virtually all our activities and relationships reflect an immensely heightened mobility—not only in our own routine physical movements but in the permanence of our places of employment, access to information, professional and other reference group memberships, sources of style and entertainment, acquisition of credit, capital and other resources, and, not least, the competition we face as a nation.

For many people, growing recognition of a wider world is accompanied less by pleasure at the discovery of new horizons than by a growing sense of vulnerability and dependency. Corporate mergers and their sometimes disastrous outcomes defy rationality and prediction. Factories break up and migrate, responding both to lower labor costs in developing countries and to declining economies of scale as assembly lines are altered by robotics and the emergence of product variability and quick turnaround as keys to competition. Sheltering careers in industrial employment have to be abandoned for the lowered incomes and insecurity of the services sector. The mismatch between the normal offerings of public education and the accelerating demands of information-oriented workplaces widens dangerously. Great urban areas fall into ruins, strangled by unemployment, suburbs, drugs, ethnic barriers.

The technological contribution to this vast series of changes has obviously been fundamental, but it is important to distinguish a marvelously enabling series of discoveries from the social arrangements that have distorted and constrained how and for whose benefit they were deployed. The clouds model of explanation, not the clock model, is the one that applies, and pride in their achievements need not lead engineers to claim an excessive share of responsibility for what is widely perceived not as progress but as loss. After all, some of the principal thrusts of development pioneered by generations of engineers have experienced a similar reversal. Economies of scale, centralization, and even standardization, long and tirelessly sought for, have virtually lost their relevance. Even labor productivity may be losing its former importance, as "much more innovative effort in the future will be directed at saving resources and energy, or substituting more abundant, but more difficult to convert and use, resources for relatively rare, but easier to convert and use, resources" (Brooks, 1980, p. 74).

All of these new parameters of change may or may not ultimately contribute to the goal of greater human welfare and—perhaps according to one's value preference!—either harmony with or mastery over nature. In a world still as full of desperate needs as this one is, I am personally inclined to be skeptical of anything that does not at least sustain industrial output and modestly advance productivity. But that engineers have had only a modest hand in the huge, complex, and still largely obscure array of forces responsible for engineering of the present state of affairs needs to be communicated to the public at every opportunity.

There is another respect in which linear, reductionist approaches do a disservice to an improved public understanding and successful implementation of sociotechnical systems. It has to do with how they are communicated and adopted, or, in processual terms, with what is known of the diffusion of innovations. This field of research has undergone an important shift in recent years, away from being conceptualized primarily as the overcoming of physical and other barriers to communications. That approach had left to the ultimate adopter of the new technology a presumably free rein of choice over his or her decision, and paid only indirect attention to the manner and effectiveness of communication to that firm or individual. Technical and even sociotechnical personnel thus played little part in demonstrating the advantages of their discoveries and devising ways to extend their use, turning this function over to marketing and advertising specialists.

Unaccounted for by this approach were the typically long lags and other discontinuities between major inventions and their successful introduction into either industrial or commercial applications. Even less well explained were frequent impediments to technology transfer that substantially distort or delay processes of economic development. Meanwhile, there has been rapid growth in sophistication about the nature and transfer of information.

Information, all would now agree, is a complex amalgam of many components with different properties. It cannot be understood as a unitary commodity that will trigger a desired decision when made available in appropriate amounts. Cultural values sometimes may be interposed, as may be also considerations of unintelligibility, trust, status anxiety, or perceived but unexpressed risk and uncertainty. Under modern conditions we face "an increasing mismatch between the complexity of the product and the ability of the purchaser to assess its qualities and performance. Thus the traditional model of the market in which producers and consumers bargain rationally, based on complete information regarding the properties of the products in question, breaks down" (Brooks, 1980, p. 74).

Adoption choices, whether by firms or individuals, of course remain a critical subject of concern. But they are now recognized not to be matters of uncontrolled free choice but of decisions made within constraint-sets that are largely imposed by widely varying conditions of access and information. Considerable research on the diffusion of innovations accordingly is being redirected toward the comparative efficacy of supply-side measures. That shifts the focus of managerial planning toward the strategic positioning, staffing, and equipping of agencies in the diffusion process (Brown, 1981, pp. 5–10). To contribute effectively to this process requires a contextual understanding of broadly interacting sociotechnical systems, and the training and working horizons of engineers need to expand accordingly.

To illustrate the extent to which adoption of new technology is not a matter of unconstrained free choice, let us briefly consider the industrialization of the home. It may appear that little more is at work here than perpetually rising expectations and discretionary income, met by a consequent satisfying of rising consumer demand with new, labor-saving technologies. And indeed there has been as sustained and profound a transformation in labor-saving efficiency in homes during the nineteenth and twentieth centuries as in most concurrent industrial advances where it is much more celebrated. Yet this outcome results, in a persuasively revisionist historian's view, from many social processes over which householders had very little direct control:

> Nowadays, the general expansion of both the economy and the welfare system has led fewer people than ever before into the market for paid domestic labor; and the diffusion of appliances into households, and of households into suburbs, has encouraged the disappearance of various commercial services. The end result is that housewives, even of the most comfortable classes (in our now generally comfortable population) are doing their housework themselves. Similarly, the extension of schooling for those who are young, the proliferation of school-related activities, and the availability of jobs for those who have finished their schooling has led to the disappearance of even those helpers upon whom the poverty-stricken housewife had once been able to depend. Hence, in almost all economic sectors of the population (except the very, very rich) housework has become manual labor (Cowan, 1983, pp. 196–197).

Most labor-saving devices, in effect, have facilitated a rescheduled and reorganized work program, without substantially reducing the hours of work that a household requires. Hence,

> The washing machine, the dishwasher, and the frozen meal have not been *causes* of married women's participation in the workforce, but they have been *catalysts* of this participation: they have acted, in the same way that chemical catalysts do, to break certain bonds that might otherwise have impeded the process. . . . Modern household technology facilitated married women's workforce participation not by freeing women from household labor but by making it possible for women to maintain decent standards in their

homes without assistance and without a full-time commitment to housework
(Cowan, 1983, pp. 208–210).

This, I submit, needs to be recognized as a new and decisive feature of our
social landscape, both incorporating and redirecting the tide of sociotechnical
advance. Engineers and designers need to deepen their own understanding of
this changing climate of demand, rather than to concede responsibility for basic
strategies of responsive management to others who lack the requisite technical
insights.

HUMAN PROGRESS

Earlier I touched momentarily on progress. Surely this idea is heavily
freighted with cultural values, not least those associated with engineering. So
it is noteworthy that not much is heard about human progress these days. As
individuals or organizations, we may "make progress," but earlier aspirations
for progress as a realizable goal for large social aggregates—for nation states,
let alone the community of nations—are mired in skepticism if not outright
disbelief. This is a time of concern instead with the unintended and perverse
effects of ambitious, large-scale efforts to deal with almost any challenge or
problem, prominently including "runaway" science and technology.

The confidence that was generally projected into the future as recently as
a generation ago was in large part associated with the assumption of indefinitely continuing improvements in our quality of life. The characteristically
overreaching optimism of the time was captured in Alvin Weinberg's emphasis
on quick technological palliatives or "fixes" (1967, p. 416) that somehow all
fell well short of their objectives. Many of the associated innovations are now
widely regarded as having been at least partly vitiated by shortsightedness and
miscalculation over the environment. Do we trace this to the eruption of a
new set of values, or to lessons of vulnerability repeatedly hammered home by
intervening decades of more doubtful experience? Does it matter which? The
ways in which we can go forward to establish a new consensus are the same in
any case.

Similarly, there was confidence a generation ago in what seemed the natural
ascendancy of this country based on the technological primacy it had achieved.
Admittedly this had occurred in a context of massive military destruction from
which we had largely escaped, but the prodigious success of our own wartime
efforts seemed to suggest no limit to what could be attained through self-
sustaining technological progress alone. Now we may think we know better,
but is this because our values have altered or because any slow turn of the
historical wheel will inevitably highlight—for a time—new risks, opportunities,
and experiences? As a frank partisan of materialistic progress, I am less
disturbed by the rise of spirited opposition to it, at least sustaining an interest

in the issue, than by the concomitant growth of a narrow preoccupation with the here-and-now.

Early in American history, I might note, there was little recognition of a potential conflict between a widely professed love of nature and the ambition to become an industrial power. These attitudes, now regarded by many as incompatible, somehow harmonized to form a single vision of the fulfillment of our national destiny (Kasson, 1976, p. 174). It was only in the later nineteenth century that a gradual shift can be traced, principally in the darkening tones of literary imagery connected with industrialism and its products (Marx, 1964). Since then, of course, the attack on a dehumanizing, engulfing technocratic mastery has broadened and become more direct, as exemplified in the works of Aldous Huxley, Charles Chaplin, George Orwell, Kurt Vonnegut, and others. In many domains of the social sciences and humanities as well, "the technocratic image is now associated with a political pathology" (Gunnell, 1982, p. 397). I do not mean to minimize the strength of these forces. With the growing depth of their own historical traditions, their movement has acquired self-sustaining autonomy as well as numbers and momentum.

But in the end, what means have we of improving the common life and overcoming its many adversities, other than scientific-technical and sociotechnical ones? There is a good case for broadening the managerial, analytical, and communications skills of engineers, particularly in sociotechnical areas. Greater concern for identifying and mitigating the adverse human impacts of technological innovations is badly needed. But engineering as a profession may not abandon its mission. As Daniel Boorstin, the former Librarian of Congress, observed not long ago,

> To fail to do all that we can is to fail to be human. . . . The point is, man is not free not to elaborate his technology. He must pursue the path that he sees but has never followed (Boorstin, 1986, pp. 102, 130).

REFERENCES

Boorstin, D. 1986. Interview. Omni 8(May):102–130 (passim).

Brooks, H. 1980. Technology, evolution, and purpose. Daedalus 109:65–81.

Brown, L. A. 1981. Innovation Diffusion: A New Perspective. London: Methuen.

Cowan, R. S. 1983. More Work for Mother: The Ironies of Household Technology from the Open Hearth to the Microwave. New York: Basic Books.

Douglas, M. 1990. Risk as a forensic resource. Daedalus 119(4):1–16.

Freudenburg, W. R. 1988. Perceived risk, real risk: Social science and the art of probabilistic risk assessment. Science 242.44–49.

Gunnell, J. G. 1982. The technocratic image and the theory of technocracy. Technology and Culture 23:392–416.

Kasson, J. F. 1976. Civilizing the Machine: Technology and Republican Values in America 1776-1900. New York: Grossman.

Marx, L. 1964. The Machine in the Garden: Technology and the Pastoral Ideal in America. New York: Oxford University Press.

Sills, D. L. 1984. The trouble with technology. Nature 309:185.

Simon, H. 1981. The Sciences of the Artificial, 2nd ed. Cambridge, Mass.: MIT Press.

Slovic, P. 1987. Perception of risk. Science 236:280–285.

Teuber, A. 1990. Justifying risk. Daedalus 119(4):235–254.

Tschinkel, V. J. 1989. The rise and fall of environmental expertise. Pp. 159–166 in Technology and Environment, J. H. Ausubel and H. E. Sladovich, eds. Washington, D.C.: National Academy Press.

Weinberg, A. M. 1967. Social problems and national socio-technical institutes. Pp. 415–434 in Applied Science and Technological Progress, A report to the Committee on Science and Astronautics, U.S. House of Representatives. Washington, D.C.: National Academy of Sciences.

Wildavsky, A., and K. Dake. 1990. Theories of risk perception: Who fears what and why? Daedalus 119(4):41–60.

2
Organizational Perspectives

Business, Consumers, and Society-at-Large: New Demands and Expectations

MARINA v.N. WHITMAN

The engineer in America today is looked to for solutions to a seemingly endless array of problems that go far beyond what can be found in the textbooks that were part of his or her formal training. Business leaders look to engineers for answers to the competitive challenges confronting them; consumers look to them for more convenient, affordable, reliable, and value-laden products; and government leaders and public interest groups look to them for technological solutions to societal concerns such as safety, health, energy conservation, and protection of the environment. The focus is especially intense because the three constituencies overlap: the consumer is also a voter, the business executive is also a consumer, as is the government official or politician, and there is frequently tension between his or her interests and goals in each role.

In short, engineering is in the spotlight as never before. While it is true that the profession has always served all three constituencies (business, consumers, and society-at-large) and advanced all of their goals, the intensity of the demands and expectations focused upon the engineering profession and the individual engineer from all three directions today is truly unprecedented.

The intensity of those demands and expectations is related to what has emerged as a national crisis of confidence, stemming from the convergence of several unprecedented trends over the past decade or so. The United States has shifted from trade surplus to chronic deficit and from the world's largest international creditor to its largest international debtor. At the same time, we have seen the end of U.S. economic hegemony, with Japan challenging our industrial leadership and such countries as Singapore, Taiwan, South Korea, and Hong Kong—the "Four Tigers"—achieving high rates of manufacturing productivity and economic growth by combining relatively inexpensive labor with modern technology. Symptoms of the resulting confidence crisis include the erosion of our postwar sense of responsibility for maintaining effective international trade and monetary systems and the gradual shift in self-identity that comes with a feeling that we can no longer afford to sublimate short-term economic interests to longer-run strategic and foreign policy goals.

The question of "What happened to us, and why?" has been the focus of seemingly endless debate and a string of news stories about where the country's weaknesses lie and how the priorities should be set for industry as well as government. The caliber of America's engineering has been featured prominently in the debate and in the articles because anxiety over industrial competitiveness has emerged as one of the most prominent symptoms of our faltering self-confidence.

Why are engineering and the engineer now perceived to be at the heart of both the problem and the solution? It is because of a widespread sense that our competitive problem is more one of the effective application of scientific knowledge (i.e., technology transfer) than of inadequacy in basic scientific innovation. The argument is that America remains a leader in basic scientific innovation but that we have fallen down in the industrial and commercial application of those innovations. Japan's technological and industrial success over the past three decades, it is generally believed, has been in application rather than innovation: the Japanese have mastered the art of taking the scientist's innovation and then engineering new or improved commercial applications for it. One of the most vivid examples, of course, is the videocassette recorder. The technology was developed in this country but the Japanese made it commercial. Today there are no VCRs built in this country.

The situation is especially ironic because of what is happening in the education and training of engineers. The world's leading postgraduate programs in science and engineering are here in this country, but they are increasingly filled by students from abroad because so many Americans apparently lack the training, the desire, or both to fill them.

All of this points to the need to raise the status, understanding, and recognition of the engineering profession. At the same time, of course, the same demands and expectations that are now focused on the engineer also underscore the need to raise engineers' own understanding of the complexity of the demands that confront them and to raise their ability to communicate effectively with nonengineers: all of which again underscores the need for nonengineers to appreciate the role of engineering in our society. In this paper, I will first explore the nature of the demands and expectations being put on the engineer in three different aspects: the product, the manufacturing process, and the workplace. I will then explore the implications of these demands for the skills needed by engineers as we approach the twenty-first century. Most of the examples used throughout the paper come from the auto industry but all have general application to the engineering profession.

PRODUCT DEMANDS AND EXPECTATIONS IN THE AUTO INDUSTRY

Demands and expectations relative to products are at the heart of the engineer's daily challenge and thus warrant more detailed analysis than those relative to the manufacturing process and the workplace. The traditional demands to engineer an automobile that will satisfy the consumer have been complicated by newer demands to further a wide variety of *social* goals that include promoting safety and preserving the environment. At the same time, the traditional demands for an automobile that is cost-effective and state-of-the-art—in short, one that will help the engineer's firm remain competitive by meeting customer demands—have been intensified by the globalization of competition and the accelerated pace and diffusion of technological change.

Global Economic Interdependence and Competition

The globalization of competition, often discussed in the context of our national crisis of confidence with the exchange of buzzwords rather than the analysis of fundamental forces, deserves special note. The globalization of competition is in fact both a cause and an effect of a shift toward global economic interdependence, a phenomenon that is beyond the control of the engineer, the economist, or the politician, and yet is shaped in part by all of them.

From the perspective of the engineer, seeking to get a grip on the opportunities as well as the problems that come with a global marketplace, there are two crucial aspects of interdependence: one positive and one negative—not unlike yin and yang in the Confucian view of the world. The positive aspect is expansion of international trade and investment stimulate economic growth and development. That was certainly true during the quarter century following World War II, when growth in trade and investment stimulated steady increases in output, income, and living standards around the globe.

But there is also a negative or "dark" aspect. As countries share in the benefits of trade and investment, they become more vulnerable to shifts and disruptions in goods and financial markets outside their borders. Unfortunately, but perhaps inevitably, this vulnerability is the aspect of interdependence that has registered most strongly in the national consciousness during the economic turbulence of the 1970s and 1980s.

At the microeconomic level, growing interdependence makes it increasingly difficult to separate domestic markets, products, and competition from international ones. Markets, competition, and production have all become global. The action is now across the world as well as across the street, with companies having to deal with international competitors in their "home" markets as well as in export markets.

What has happened in the U.S. auto industry is typical of many other industries. In 1962, imports accounted for 4 percent of the vehicles sold in the United States, compared with nearly 30 percent today. Not only are foreign-based competitors exporting to the U.S. market; they are setting up production bases to reduce the uncertainties associated with exchange rates and the threat of import restraints. For example, the Japanese have built what in the auto industry are called "transplants," plants that produce vehicles in this country to capture expanded market-share growth that would otherwise be reflected entirely in increased imports from Japan.

And, of course, U.S. manufacturers have also been placing increasing importance on markets and production bases outside North America. Exchange rates, relative production costs, and the size of foreign markets themselves have led U.S. automakers to global marketing and production strategies using a variety of locations for component production and vehicle assembly and aimed at a variety of geographic markets.

One of the most important lessons we have learned from the competitive battle of the 1980s is that it is not a simple matter of geography, with North America destined to lose out to the Pacific Rim, as many observers thought a few years ago. High-quality and high-value automobiles can be produced and sold in virtually any part of the globe. For example, some Japanese auto manufacturers, as well as U.S. manufacturers, are now building cars cost-effectively in this country for export to Japan.

The Need to Set World Standards

The lesson for industry and for the engineering profession is that leaders in today's global marketplace set world standards for innovation, quality, and value. They do not just meet the standards set elsewhere or set standards among domestic competitors. This high-sounding challenge is the same basic business principle that has applied ever since people began selling things to one another. The way to beat the competition and win the buyer's decision is to build better products and deliver better service at a price that the buyer perceives to give good value.

The globalization of competition has also taught us that when industries or companies cannot compete effectively in product quality and value, trade barriers or related forms of government intervention offer ephemeral solutions. They only delay the day of reckoning for those domestic firms that fail to meet or exceed the foreign competition's standards.

Similar examples of the integration of service and high-technology activities and expertise into traditional manufacturing and products abound in other industries. In fact, it would be inaccurate to describe "high-tech" itself as a separate industry or even a separate segment of any given industry. The forces of global competition lead all competitors in all industries—including the auto industry—to adopt state-of-the-art technology in every aspect of their operations.

The distinctions between goods and services are similarly diminishing. Indeed, one leading financial analyst recently observed that "already, U.S. businesses get more of their financing from General Motors than from Citicorp." This increasing consumer reliance on the financial service arms of such automotive companies as Ford and General Motors for financing is only one example of today's intertwined service and manufacturing industries. Each is often the other's customer; what happens in one affects the other. Also, in the auto industry, as in many others, success is determined by the total customer experience, not by the product alone. That means that the dealer's "service," encompassing personal treatment of the customer as well as how well the product is serviced, may be as crucial as the perceived quality and value of the product. The engineer is in a sense the point person in this process of integrating high-tech services into the manufacturing process, as will be discussed in more detail.

In the quest to set world standards, industrial companies are incorporating large elements of the so-called service and high-tech sectors into traditional manufacturing activities. For example, General Motors acquired Electronic Data Systems, an information technology services company to integrate the computer into all phases of GM's design, engineering, and manufacturing processes in facilities around the world. Similarly, one of the major goals in the acquisition of Hughes Aircraft was to apply their leadership in systems engineering and electronics to the development of today's and tomorrow's vehicles. To put all this in perspective, the market for automotive electronics, including microprocessors, is expected to grow from around $18 billion in 1990 to $30 billion by 1995, while the electronic value of an average vehicle is expected to grow from $600 today to as much as $1,500 by 1995.

Growing Societal Demands on the Product

Competitive pressures make it both more important and more difficult for the engineer to balance the demands of the customer with those of society. The automobile is a good example of the tension. The customer demands mobility, style, comfort, convenience, reliability, affordability, and value; society demands safety, fuel efficiency, and pollution reduction.

This balancing act is becoming increasingly difficult in part, because of our postwar economic success. As U.S. companies prospered and incomes and living standards rose, society began to demand an increasing measure of "nonmarket" or "social" goods—such things as safety, and environmental protection. These demands on industry and government, in turn, spawned an evermore complex regulatory environment and an uncomfortably adversarial relationship between government and business. This relationship itself has almost certainly played a role in the national crisis of confidence we are experiencing today.

A benchmark in the evolution of this uncomfortably adversarial relationship is a famous, and often-misquoted, anecdote from the 1950s, when a General Motors president made headlines and won himself a place in history at a Senate hearing. The man was "Engine Charlie" Wilson and he was testifying after being nominated as Secretary of Defense by President Eisenhower. What the newspapers quoted him as saying was, "What's good for General Motors is good for America, and vice versa." What he really said was, "I have always believed that what's good for America is good for General Motors, and vice versa."

That statement was great fodder for the critics, but it is in fact not a bad description of reality. In the big picture, when one gains the other gains, and vice versa. Clearly, the two are never going to converge on every issue. But at the same time, we cannot expect society and industry to maximize their competitive potential in the world arena if the tone of the relationship between government and business is predominantly adversarial—in contrast to the more cooperative relationships that characterize "most" other industrialized countries.

As was noted by Sheila Jasanoff in a recent issue of *Daedalus* devoted exclusively to the subject of risk (Jasanoff, 1990, p. 63):

> Studies of public health, safety, and environmental regulation published in the 1980s revealed striking differences between American and European practices for managing technological risks. These studies showed that U.S. regulators on the whole were quicker to respond to new risks, more aggressive in pursuing old ones, and more concerned with producing technical justifications for their actions than their European counterparts. Regulatory styles, too, diverged sharply somewhere over the Atlantic Ocean. The U.S. process for making risk decisions impressed all observers as costly, confrontational, litigious, formal, and unusually open to participation. European decision making, despite important differences within and among countries, seemed by comparison almost uniformly cooperative and consensual; informal, cost conscious, and for the most part closed to the public.

All of this is not to say we should adopt the kind of government subsidies or targeted national industrial strategies that are used by some of our trading partners. Rather, both sides need to be aware of the stakes involved when public policy in the form of legislative or regulatory requirements impedes, rather than harnesses, the working of market forces. One of the greatest lessons of the past 20 years of regulation is that market incentives are in most cases far more effective in achieving societal goals than regulatory mandates that attempt to command and control economic behavior.

Again, the engineering function is inevitably affected by the nature of the relationship between business and government. In the United States, engineers have had to respond to a process for setting automotive emissions standards that from the perspective of the automobile industry has often seemed to be determined more by emotion and political pressure than by either hard scientific data or the realities of the marketplace. In Western Europe, in contrast, the less adversarial climate has allowed for a more rational and cooperative approach to solutions for pollution reduction. For example, 19 European governments and 400 companies and research institutions have cooperated in funding the $4.9 billion EUREKA project for the development of Intelligent Vehicle-Highway Systems (IVHS) technologies. In the United States, in contrast, less than $10 million has been committed to the two largest IVHS projects now under way. One of these, Project PATHFINDER, is a $1.65 million cooperative venture between the California Department of Transportation, the Federal Highway Administration, and General Motors. The other, funded with $8 million is called TRAVTEK. It is a venture between the Federal Highway Administration, the American Automobile Association, the Florida Department of Transportation, the City of Orlando, Florida, and GM.

Market Incentives versus Command-and-Control Regulation: The Environmental Example

Market-based incentives are more effective in reaching technological solutions to societal problems than are command-and-control regulations. This point is especially relevant to the current debate over environmental protection. Perhaps the most important advantage of market-based approaches, from the engineer's viewpoint as well as that of the policymaker, is their ability to foster long-term innovation. Environmental policies must be structured to achieve steady, continuous improvements. To be successful, such improvements must stay ahead of economic growth to ensure that living standards keep pace with the growth of population in much of the world. To solve this Malthusian dilemma, the environmental progress of one generation simply must provide a basis for further progress in the next.

Only markets and marketlike mechanisms have this property. To be sure, command-and-control regulation can influence innovation, but the impacts are quite different. Command and control specifies maximum emissions, and often particular performance standards. This rigidity tends to limit both the scope and extent of innovation over time. It gives rise to narrowly focused changes that leave out important sectors of the economy. Such an approach also gives rise to technological change in fits and starts, as opposed to producing the kind of broad-based, steady and continuous development required for long-term innovation. Producers tend to push for only the amount of innovation necessary to achieve compliance with the standards of the day. There is no reward for exceeding those standards. Indeed, under U.S. environmental laws requiring the use of best available control technologies, the very discovery of such technologies can be grounds for further, costly technological requirements—a clear *dis*incentive for innovation.

In sharp contrast, economic incentives reward every new technology, every new production process that can result in better environmental control. Businesses have the same incentive to invest in methods and devices that reduce pollution as they do in devices that save labor or economize inputs of capital. This stimulus for producers to innovate may well be the most powerful reason for preferring market-based mechanisms over command and control for most types of pollution problems. Indeed, for global problems such as the control of greenhouse gases, where it is simply not possible to specify in advance the specific technologies that will prove to be most effective, economic incentives (as opposed to command-and-control regulation) are the best and most effective way to get "from here to there."

Costs of Environmental Progress

Concern for the environment has never been as intense or widespread as it is today. Surveys indicate that three out of four Americans consider themselves to be "environmentalists." Ninety-seven percent think the country should be doing more to protect the environment and curb pollution. Seventy-five percent say they are willing to pay higher taxes if the revenues go to cleaning up the environment.

This was the climate leading up to passage of the Clean Air Act Amendments of 1990. GM and much of the rest of U.S. industry (not just the auto industry) supported the amendments as representing a difficult stretch but also the best achievable compromise among many different interests.

However, progress—like all other things in life—has its price. The auto industry, again, provides an example of progress already achieved and challenges ahead. In the 1990s and beyond, the engineer will be a key player in the policy debate as well as the implementation of new solutions.

As a nation, we have made great progress in cleaning up the air since the 1970s, in spite of continued population and economic growth. According to the Environmental Protection Agency, ozone formation in the lower atmosphere in this country has been reduced by 21 percent; nitrogen dioxide by 14 percent; and dirt, dust, and particulates by 23 percent. The U.S. automobile industry has made major contributions to improved air quality by reducing emissions from its vehicles and its plants. Emissions from new passenger cars have been reduced substantially since clean air regulations were first introduced. There are three important categories of emissions from the vehicles on our roads today: unburned fuel in the form of hydrocarbons; partially burned fuel or carbon monoxide; and oxides of nitrogen, a by-product of the combustion process. Since the early 1970s, total exhaust emissions of hydrocarbons and carbon monoxide from passenger cars have been reduced by 96 percent, and oxides of nitrogen by 76 percent.

The industry achieved those results with several significant technological innovations. The most important was the catalytic converter, which uses platinum and rhodium as catalysts for the chemical reactions that turn hydrocarbons, carbon monoxide, and oxides of nitrogen into water and carbon dioxide. Computers control air-fuel mixture and spark in the engine for maximum power, fuel economy, and minimal emissions.

As older cars are replaced with newer models equipped with the latest emission-control technology, emissions will continue to decline at no incremental cost. Currently, 85 percent of the auto pollution comes from the oldest 50 percent of the vehicles on the road. The Environmental Protection Agency estimates that by the year 2000, as older vehicles are replaced, fleet average hydrocarbon and carbon monoxide emission levels will decline by 40 to 50 percent, and oxides of nitrogen emissions by 33 percent, from current levels.

The industry has also upgraded many of its manufacturing operations. For example, billions of dollars have been invested to construct new paint facilities or modernize existing facilities to control the release of volatile organic compounds—mostly hydrocarbon solvents—as a car is spray painted.

Having made these investments and achieved this progress, the auto industry must now focus on how to remove the remaining small percentages of exhaust emissions. In the case of hydrocarbons and carbon monoxide emissions from passenger cars, for example, all but four percent of the emissions have been removed since the 1970s. The costs and technological challenges of removing that final 4 percent will be much greater than those for the first 96 percent.

The cost and effectiveness of the Clean Air Act Amendments of 1990 remain to be seen. However, from the standpoint of industry and the engineer's role in seeking and implementing new solutions, three criteria should be followed as the process of writing regulations to implement the Act moves forward: (1) The standards should be technologically feasible; (2) there should be adequate lead time to design a new system and get ready to produce it *and* adequate phase-in time to allow orderly development of systems; and, (3) there should be time to make sure that the systems put on cars could perform under real-world conditions, so that the cars our customers were actually driving would meet the standards.

The Engineer in the Eye of the Hurricane

The Clean Air Act is just one example of how the engineer is caught in the eye of the hurricane, pulled in different directions by the conflicting demands of the individual customer, the company, and the society as reflected in legislative and regulatory requirements. It often seems as if the engineer's work is overdetermined, with more objectives to be met than there are instruments with which to meet them. The consumer wants the cleanest and healthiest environment possible but *also* wants the freedom, comfort, flexibility, and utility represented by a full range of personal transportation vehicles. Consumers in all markets, including Europe, continue to demand more performance, comfort, and convenience in the automobile. The hot-selling cars today are anything but the tiny no-frills vehicles many thought were the wave of the future during the energy scares of the 1970s.

Adding to the pressure on the engineer, the societal demands weighing against such individual consumer demands are also dynamic rather than static, as are the consumer's demands and the competitive pressures discussed earlier. Trade-offs have always been the centerpiece of the engineer's challenge, but they have become broader and more difficult. What is "environmentally correct" today, for example, is far different from what was correct 25 years ago. This is highlighted by an anecdote from Robert C. Stempel, General Motors' new chairman and chief executive officer. When Bob started his career as an engineer, the ideal to aim for was perfect engine combustion, with only two "totally benign" by-products, water and carbon dioxide. But today, with concern about global warming and the greenhouse effect, carbon dioxide, rather than being benign, may actually lie at the heart of concerns about the impact of human activity on the pace and magnitude of global warming.

No one in industry, government, or the scientific community knows whether the environmental goals now being discussed can ever be achieved *or* if they even address the basic problems effectively. California, the "trend-setter" state, illustrates the dichotomy. People have never expressed greater urgency for cleaning up the air in the Los Angeles basin, but those same people indicate by their behavior that they do not want to be told what kind of car they have to drive or when they can drive it. For example, 10 years ago Hughes Aircraft began what is probably the country's largest ride-sharing program, offering its employees a fleet of 302 vans for commuting in groups to and from work, but only 19 percent of Hughes' employees participate. Sixty percent say they would not even consider ride-sharing as an alternative to enduring the frustration of fighting Los Angeles' traffic in their own automobiles.

The Experience of the 1970s as a Guide for the 1990s

The experience of the 1970s offers a vivid lesson to public policymakers as well as to industry—and the engineer in particular—in balancing conflicting pressures and priorities. The lesson is that the emotions and assumptions of the moment must be tempered with flexibility and a long-range view subject to new scientific knowledge and changing political and economic circumstances. Engineers can and must contribute to an understanding of these basic principles.

A major U.S. policy response to the 1973 Arab oil embargo was a combination of price controls on crude oil and allocation of supplies among refiners. That hastily implemented so-called solution only created an inefficient bureaucratic maze and contributed to lines at the gasoline pumps. Similarly, the United States rushed into a synthetic fuel program that was all but dead by the end of the 1970s, with little to show for the money spent.

In retrospect, one of the greatest ironies of the 1970s was that the auto industry achieved major progress in meeting societal demands for energy conservation and pollution reduction, but was nonetheless widely perceived to be dragging its heels. At the same time, the diversion of technical and financial resources made the industry take its eye off the customer satisfaction ball, which created a vacuum into which foreign competitors moved and are now well established. Consequently, today's automotive engineer is being asked to reconcile the conflict among competitive, consumer, and societal demands through ingenious applications of technology while *avoiding* these mistakes of the 1970s.

DEMANDS AND EXPECTATIONS IN AUTOMOTIVE MANUFACTURING

The challenge in manufacturing processes, is summed up in four terms every engineer has long been familiar with: cost-effectiveness, quality, speed, and flexibility. The automotive engineer is asked to reduce the cost of producing a specific component or system (such as a bumper or a transmission) while at the same time increasing the quality and reliability of the product, reducing the time required to get it to market, and making the manufacturing process more adaptable to changes in design or production volume.

Simplicity, expressed in the concept of design-for-manufacturability, has become the hallmark of virtually all engineering programs and projects today. This means the engineer must get involved in all aspects of the product cycle—from design to service and deal with a broad array of disciplines in each phase of the cycle, which is what simultaneous engineering is all about. The ideas and interests of every discipline (e.g., designers, financial and marketing experts, product and process engineers) must be taken into consideration at the beginning of the process, rather than taking a completed product design and "throwing it over the transom" to the engineers and others responsible for actual manufacturing.

The Importance of Systems Engineering

Along with simultaneous engineering, systems engineering has taken on new urgency as cost effectiveness and flexibility continue to drive the entire product cycle. Intensifying competition and the increasing complexity of the product itself are causing the industry to turn to the methodology of systems engineering for planning, executing, and validating applications of new technology.

The term "systems engineering" itself is becoming a buzzword in circles beyond the engineering profession. Like other buzzwords, however, it is sometimes used without much consideration of what it really means. Systems engineering is a cost-effective way to define, integrate and design all subsystems so that the total system design for a product best suits the original requirements.

Systems engineering starts with the definition of the customer's requirements and proceeds through the allocation of those requirements to the total system, subsystems and, finally, components of the product. All of the requisite disciplines and different organizations are pulled together at the beginning and continue working together throughout all phases as the design develops: that is, as the components, subsystems and systems, are built, integrated, and then validated against the original requirements, each component and each process phase is treated as part of the greater *system* rather than in isolation.

Not surprisingly, systems engineering methodology was developed in the defense and aerospace industries as products became more complex and customers' requirements became more stringent. In those industries, quality and overall performance had to be ensured *before* single components or subsystems could be tested as part of the total system. Without such structured coordination, this country's program to land a man on the moon might never have gotten off the ground in the 1960s. The same may apply to automotive programs in the 1990s and beyond as technology and the product itself continue to grow more sophisticated and complex.

There was a time, of course, when the automotive engineer didn't see a need for that kind of up-front discipline in planning and managing his projects. In fact, the auto industry itself evolved as a loose network of subsystems and components—an axle operation here, a gear operation there, and an engine operation in a third place, for example. Indeed, innovations at the component level have been hallmarks of our progress in such components as the electric starter and the automatic transmission, where the vehicle manufacturer brought the different units together, assembled the different subsystems, and *then* worked out the bugs.

Searching for a "perfect" solution without regard to time or cost requirement has no place in today's competitive world. As automotive subsystems and components move in the direction of much more complexity and interaction, their influence on the whole car is more pervasive. That means sophisticated new technologies such as active suspension, antilock brakes, and traction control all must be applied in harmony, as a system, if they are to fulfill their customer-satisfaction potential.

Without the systems engineering approach, making changes is costly in terms of product quality and financial expense. Hence, simultaneous engineering, with multidisciplinary focus on the customer's requirements at each stage of the design, development, and manufacturing process, must go hand-in-hand with systems engineering.

DEMANDS AND EXPECTATIONS
IN THE AUTOMOTIVE WORKPLACE

Demands and expectations placed on the engineer today have been heightened by changes in the workplace itself, as well as in product and process. The movement toward participative management in the past few years means that the engineer's attitudes and perspectives on his or her own role in the organization have to shift.

There is a renewed emphasis on the central role of people and human relationships in the bottom line. The old hierarchical or adversarial structure of authority is giving way to more cooperative, consensus-based, decentralized authority models. This shift away from traditional labor relations to what might better be called "workplace relations" reflects changing individual values and greater educational and skill requirements, shown first by Japanese and Swedish manufacturers as examples of successful employee involvement and participatory management to drive competitive advantage.

At the same time, however, change in the hierarchical authority structure does *not* imply abrogation of management's own responsibilities to provide leadership and produce a favorable return on the stockholders' investment. Rather, it implies a different, more open and consultative style of leadership. General Motors, like scores of other major companies, has implemented several changes to facilitate this different style. One GM example is a joint labor-management process called the Quality Network, meant to make a core set of beliefs and values the way of life throughout the workplace. The Quality Network's beliefs and values are customer satisfaction through people, teamwork, and continuous improvement.

Managers and engineers alike can no longer expect to get the best results by issuing commands and analyzing requirements and results in black-and-white terms. Traditional lines of authority are blurring not only in reaction to individual needs for self-fulfillment but also because American business has witnessed and analyzed a number of foreign models (particularly in Japan and Sweden) in which less authoritarianism and more employee involvement have led to success in the marketplace.

The growing diversity of the work force itself also poses new challenges to management style and practices, as was highlighted in the landmark *Workforce 2000* study conducted by the Hudson Institute for the U.S. Department of Labor (1987). The following are among the study's major conclusions:

- Native-born white males will make up only 15 percent of the new entrants into the labor force between 1987 and the year 2000, compared with the traditional rate of more than 50 percent.
- Nonwhites will account for nearly 30 percent of the new entrants into the work force between 1987 and the year 2000, compared with less than 15 percent two years ago.
- Almost two-thirds of the new entrants into the work force between 1987 and the year 2000 will be women.
- Nonwhites, immigrants, and women together will make up more than 83 percent of the net additions to the work force, compared with about 50 percent today.

Culturally diverse employees and consumers want to buy products or services from companies sensitive to their wants and needs. They also seek adequate representation in professional and managerial positions, as well as at other levels in the company's work force.

U.S. business will increasingly aim its products and services at women and minorities at the same time as it relies on women and minorities to produce and sell those products and services. That is why one of the major challenges facing U.S. business today is to make sure future workers are given competitive education and training *before* they enter the workplace as well as throughout their working years. The way that challenge is met will affect management and organizational styles and effectiveness (i.e., the "business culture") in all firms.

The definition of manager and engineer (as well as other specialists) in the corporation is also changing. Peter Drucker, the dean of management theorists, has predicted that the combined impact of mergers and acquisitions and the increasing need for specialized skills will lead to a drastic reduction in "middle" and "upper" management ranks between now and the year 2000 (Drucker, 1988). In his view, more and more managers will be performing technical or specialized production or marketing-related work rather than "general" management functions, and many "professional" people will be earning more money than the managers to whom they report!

All this applies also to the engineering profession—only more so—because it is at the center of the process of developing, refining, and making marketable the product that is the heart of the business. The engineer's rising prominence in the workplace will also be heightened by what is often called a "back to the basics" movement in the business world. There is less emphasis on diversification, more scrutiny of the reasons for foreign competitors' success, and a general reappraisal of the fundamentals in all industries. This has led to renewed emphasis on the processes of providing goods and services to the customer rather than shuffling assets: a focus on "work" rather than "deals." Engineering and manufacturing are fashionable again!

TWO CRITICAL TOOLS OF MODERN ENGINEERING PRACTICE

Two tools that were not always seen as essential to get the job done in the past are now crucial for the engineer.

Lifelong learning and retraining The very uncertainty and dynamism of world circumstances require ongoing lifelong education rather than a process that ends with the receipt of the diploma. The pace of technological change, the growing internationalization and interdependence of markets, and the growing intensity of competition in most industries dictate that education and training be a constant process. The young engineer leaving school and entering the job market 20 years ago might well have assumed that the combination of the degree he or she was about to receive plus a capacity for hard work would be a sure ticket for career success and job security. However, no one entering the profession can make that assumption today with industry's emphasis on simultaneous engineering and system engineering.

Similarly, engineering training itself cannot be limited to its traditional curriculum. The disciplines of science and engineering are both growing more complex and intertwined as the knowledge base expands.

The engineer needs to understand other disciplines involved in the product, process, and workplace in order to make the trade-offs and achieve the balance discussed in this paper. The trade-offs and balancing act go beyond purely engineering assessments of which kind of sensor or fastener to use in specific product applications. They involve design and marketing disciplines related to customer satisfaction, and they involve economic and political analysis related to competitive and social goals and the legislative and regulatory process. The engineer needs to understand the interaction between engineering considerations and the much broader societal trade-offs confronting business today.

In the regulatory arena, for example, several tough nonengineering questions have to be answered and balanced against one another. The engineer plays a crucial role in finding the answers. For example:

- What is the degree of scientific uncertainty associated with regulatory proposals?
- Can the targets be achieved, given current technology? If not, what effect is "technology-forcing" likely to have?
- Will the proposals in fact have the intended effect if carried out?
- What are the ultimate costs and benefits of the proposals?
- Which problems require global solutions, and which are better answered by local solutions?
- What will it take to induce American consumers to pay the price? For example, will they be willing to buy an alternative-fuel vehicle if the industry is forced by legislation or regulation to build it?

We still do not know the answers to these questions, but they *must* be answered and balanced against each other as well as against the common goal of a healthier environment.

Systems engineering can be an invaluable aid in the quest for this balance, and engineers can make a tremendous contribution to society if they take it upon themselves to include policymakers in such thinking. Public policy, not unlike an automobile or airplane, is the sum of separate laws and regulations.

It is not enough that individual proposals make sense on their own merits: for the resulting policy to be effective, hundreds of separate proposals, laws, and regulations must reinforce and mesh with each other into a coherent, manageable whole rather than duplicate, complicate, or hinder each other.

In government, several different congressional committees and regulatory agencies are responsible for formulating and enforcing public policy regarding safety, clean air, and energy. Constraints on time and other resources, combined with the overlapping jurisdictions of the various committees and agencies, make it difficult for each to analyze fully what the other is doing. The result can be a set of laws and regulations that may appear to be well focused, but when examined individually add up to confusing, unintendedly burdensome, and even self-contradictory policy. Strict adherence to the systems engineering approach enhance the policymaking process as well as the end product (and would make life simpler for all).

Communication skills   Because the engineer's skill and judgment are sought out and scrutinized by a wide variety of constituencies, from manufacturing experts to marketing experts to public interest groups and government, today's engineer must be able to speak and *write* clearly, precisely, and persuasively. The warning issued by C. P. Snow (1959) in *The Two Cultures* is more valid today than ever. He warned that scientists and nonscientists were building a wall between themselves by their inability to understand each other's jargon, to the detriment of both groups as well as society at large.

That danger is even greater today. If the scientist and engineer do not communicate precisely and easily, if they do not understand each other's language and each other's world, then how can they be effective in dealing with the customers, public interest groups, and government officials who are demanding so much of them? It is interesting indeed that Snow's treatise is appearing more and more frequently in speeches and articles on environmental and other regulatory issues.

Internally, the combination of interdisciplinary approaches and projects (e.g., simultaneous engineering and systems engineering) and more participative management means that engineers must be effective communicators with those above them (management) and those around them (peers in engineering and other disciplines). Externally, changing societal demands and expectations focused on engineers also mean that they must be effective communicators with those looking in on them (news media, legislators, regulators, public interest groups). They must be able to explain the need for cooperative, nonadversarial approaches and relationships both internally and externally.

That means engineers must understand the thinking, goals, and constraints of "the other side" before they communicate their own views on an issue or problem. Again, C. P. Snow's argument is relevant. There is a vast difference between what the word "possible" means to the engineer and what it means to the regulator. For the engineer, "possible" means there is a good chance, though not a certainty, of being able to accomplish a goal: once it is accomplished, it must then be validated, certified, and worked into the product cycle.

For the regulator, on the other hand, when someone says a goal is "possible" it is often taken to mean that it can be implemented in a short time frame, meet certification requirements, and remain durable under a sweeping array of operating conditions—on pain of recall or fines. Engineers must understand this difference if we are to have a regulatory framework that takes account of technological feasibility, adequate lead time, and an orderly phase-in process, all of which are essential for quality and product assurance under real-world conditions.

At the same time, of course, engineers cannot afford to let themselves be intimidated or paralyzed by such differences in perception; they must maintain a traditional willingness to stretch, reach, and take risks. If they lose that willingness, then the continuous innovation that is the lifeblood of any dynamic society will inevitably suffer.

CONCLUSION

The future course of U.S. business and the U.S. economy will be determined by the interaction of three powerful forces: technological advances, competitive pressure to respond to consumer demands, and social expectations as embodied in legislative and regulatory requirements. Engineers, who have always been deeply involved in technological change are increasingly called on to respond to the other two forces as well. This implies increased leverage, broader opportunities, and more complex challenges for engineers, requiring in turn new skills, greater flexibility, and a broader perspective. As business, the individual consumer, and society work together to balance conflicting demands and make difficult trade-offs, it is clear that engineering will increasingly become a "social enterprise" as we move toward the twenty-first century.

REFERENCES

Drucker, P. 1988. Tomorrow's restless managers. Industry Week. April 18, pp. 25–26.
Jasanoff, S. 1990. American Exceptionalism and the Political Acknowledgement of Risk. Daedalus 119(4):61–81.
Snow, C. P. 1959. The Two Cultures and the Scientific Revolution. The Rede Lecture. New York: Cambridge University Press.
U.S. Department of Labor. 1987. Workforce 2000: Work and Workers for the 21st Century. Washington, D.C.: U.S. Government Printing Office.

Technology and Government

JOHN W. FAIRCLOUGH

Technology's positive contribution to society grows remorselessly, and the engineering enterprise provides an essential contribution in terms of the functioning of the market. One need only compare the success of the market economies in bringing new technologies on stream with the dismal record of the East European economies to see the deadening effect of the ideological approach.

This paper examines the factors that influence the way governments handle technology. My experience in both the public and the private sectors has led me to some conclusions about the role of government in the encouragement and exploitation of science and technology and its contribution to the collective wealth of nations in three central areas: the interaction between industry and science, the role of government as regulator and major procurement agency, and the influence of financial institutions and economic factors. Moreover, the role of public opinion in shaping decisions in each of these three areas implies responsibilities for scientists and engineers to become better communicators about their work.

INTERACTIONS BETWEEN INDUSTRY AND SCIENCE

The fundamental objectives of national governments are the security and the prosperity of their citizens. This applies to postindustrial economies in the last decade of the twentieth century just as it did to countries with democratically elected governments a century ago.

Today, technology is still seen as a liberator to the same degree that it replaced the inhuman factory conditions in the sweat shops during the first industrial revolution. It has the power to transform routine, boring, and dangerous tasks, elevate the individual to loftier pursuits, and save lives. But technology's contribution to corporate results, rather than its enhancement of quality of life, is now widely perceived as its prime task. Economics seems to have taken over as the driving force of technology, with productivity and profitability assuming the dominant role.

The technological and scientific vitality of a country is of increasing concern to governments. It is no coincidence that the electorate judge governments on their economic record. To get elected, let alone reelected, governments need comprehensive policies in education, training, health care, defense, environment, and transport infrastructure—sectors where technology and its application play a fundamental role and are seen as a panacea.

National governments, like companies, face the reality that economic competitiveness in the international marketplace is essential, and not just for countries such as the United Kingdom, which have been traditionally dependent on trading. The principle applies across the board. It affects high-technology products as much as traditional manufacturing industries. Technology is the common thread determining success or failure in the service sector, an important component of all economies, and manufacturing. Economic prosperity, technology, and quality of life are accordingly inextricably linked.

In these circumstances, it is now accepted wisdom that the successful exploitation of technology is a prerequisite for strong economic performance and the generation of wealth and resources needed to provide services demanded by taxpayers. It is equally observable that governments are becoming more active in examining initiatives to support the formation of competitive technologies and assessing the relative resources required for science. Even the United States government, which has tended to play a somewhat limited role in formulating technology policy, is considering such initiatives.

There are generally thought to be two main fountains of technology: scientific discovery and industrial innovation. In my view there is a third, possibly even more important mechanism: the flow of new ideas between industry and the academic community. This relationship is not without tensions. The interaction will prosper only if there is a receptive attitude by industry and fertile ground for academic initiative. Industry has to foster such an attitude by posing academics with fundamental scientific challenges that contribute both to the future success of industry and a better targeting of academic work. Absent this mutually reinforcing process, the academic community will be tempted to undertake work that bears little relevance to industrial commercialization. The question of a nation's ability to pay for such an unselective approach to technology innovation cannot be ignored.

In my view, industry sometimes fails to recognize its own self-interest in this regard by neglecting a responsibility to specify its requirements for scientific and technological research in such a way that maintains and develops academic excellence. Corporate endowment of universities and institutions is to be welcomed. But many industrial chairmen believe their duty extends no further than charity. This surely is subsidiary to ensuring the existence of an intellectual partnership, which is infinitely more valuable to both universities and industry than mere charity alone.

Governments' first duty is to ensure that academia is awarded its fair share of public money with complete freedom to pursue intellectually interesting fields of scientific inquiry. Governments then need to be satisfied that resources for targeted work, where commercialization is the goal, are supported by sound industrial underpinning where setting priorities is essential for judging the relevance, rather than scientific excellence, of the proposed research. In the United Kingdom, outside chemistry and the life sciences, we have a standoff: industry says it cannot rely on academia because of lengthy time horizons and an inability to apply multidisciplinary skills or work to a schedule; academia's reaction is to claim public money to work on every promising field!

Within industry conflicting pressures include the tug toward self-sufficiency in technology to protect long-term competitiveness and the temptation to renounce substantial in-house research and license know-how and technology. The inescapable fact is that almost no company can expect to master directly all the technologies to which it needs access. It must depend on the flow of ideas, patents, and intellectual property to ensure a complete portfolio. Only by balancing these conditions can international competitiveness and a margin of superiority be achieved. All this underlines the fundamental importance of an effective relationship between industry and the academic community. It is partly the responsibility of government to ensure that this constitutes a virtuous circle of cooperation, not a dialogue of the deaf. However, governments cannot enforce a change of attitudes; it is up to the participants themselves to be mutually reinforcing. The lead must come from industry, not simply with money, but with a statement of future needs expressed in terms that capture the imagination of academia.

ROLE OF GOVERNMENT AS REGULATOR AND MAJOR PROCUREMENT AGENCY

Governments purchase huge quantities of equipment and services. In doing so they can provide leadership and inspire the development of new technology to serve their requirements while also reinforcing the competitiveness of their national industries. At the same time they may unwittingly act as a cushion for complacent industry. The "beltway bandit" is not a species unique to the United States.

There may be something of a contradiction between governments' natural caution in pursuing value for money and the element of risk taking essential to promoting technological innovation. Although governments need to guard against buying unproven and potentially unworkable technologies—the graveyards are full of monuments to such white elephants—they also need to avoid simple dependence on "easy" or obsolescent technology.

The thesis that defense procurement is a primary source of commercial spin-offs in the civil sector has been largely exploded. Indeed, technologies that underpin defense systems are increasingly derived from civil development work where the necessary economy of scale for introduction to the marketplace obtains. New materials and electronics, for example, are rarely driven by defense specifications even if certain products need to be custom designed. The new situation in Europe seems likely to bring further changes in the defense technology sector as the imperative for companies to diversify reduces the technology push from defense to civil applications.

That is not to say that the flow of technology from defense to civil applications should be underestimated. The record of the Defense Advanced Research Projects Agency in the United States shows what can be done. This organization has made an admirable contribution to the recognition of dual use technologies. This trend toward developing dual-use technology, however, has put some governments in a difficult position. For example, in the United Kingdom the Ministry of Defence is required by Parliament to show that every penny is exclusively devoted to the defense purpose, making it hard to be associated with dual-use technologies. This is an area where governments need to step up their efforts.

Regulatory Environment

One of the most potent ways governments can stimulate technological innovation is by creating a favorable regulatory climate. Regulation is intended to protect the individual, to ensure effective competition, and to control the social consequences of industrial processes. The control of emissions from large power generating plants or the replacement of polluting processes by cleaner technologies are areas where government influence is seen as positive and benign. It is no coincidence that those countries with tough environmental regulations also have well-developed environmental technologies. Information technology and electronic communications services offer another example of technology development sensitive to regulatory frameworks. When the first generation of mobile telephones was developed in Europe, a series of incompatible systems were introduced in 12 European Community (EC) countries. Agreement on a common standard for the next generation will mean freedom of speech from the Atlantic to the Urals will take on a new and literal connotation! It is also notable that liberalization or deregulation of electronic communication in the United States, Japan, and the United Kingdom has led to greater expansion of telecommunications and data networks than in France or Germany, where state monopolies maintain more rigid control. The whole area of standards is one where the is EC taking on a key role through collaborative prenormative research by the member states. Much of the EC R&D Framework Programme is devoted to establishing common standards in such fields as telecommunication and computing networks, new materials and their routine testing, medical drugs and pesticide testing, and so on. A European Single Market will be achieved only through standards normalization, and the EC is already proving to be a highly effective negotiating forum and enforcement agency in such work.

Governments also need to regulate to take account of public opinion. In doing so, however, it may act as a brake on innovation. Nuclear energy is a classic example. Following Three Mile Island, Chernobyl, and other accidents, the French, and to a lesser extent the Japanese, have retained confidence in a large-scale nuclear energy program. Elsewhere the termination of major investments in nuclear capacity, despite its attractiveness in terms of CO_2 emissions, has been the direct consequence of eroding public confidence in a technology and its management. Governments alone are probably powerless to reverse such attitudes. It is the responsibility of business enterprises and the engineering profession to match public expectations of inherent safety design and to show that this dominates the design selection rather than the strictly technical need for maximum efficiency. In a paper entitled "Engineering in an Age of Anxiety," Alvin M. Weinberg (1989) discusses this subject with great eloquence. It will take many years for the nuclear power industry to recover from its relentless devotion to the kilowatt-per-dollar equation rather than the pursuit of public confidence in fail-safe measures.

By contrast, public attitudes toward biotechnology and genetic manipulation are still being formed. We are at a crucial stage. Although we have seen considerable progress with the application of these techniques for diagnostic kits, there is growing fear of these genetically engineered materials entering the food chain either directly or indirectly by herbicides and pesticides. This public concern is probably more highly developed in Germany where, for example, a major German company had to abandon a significant investment in a biotechnology process to produce insulin for human application. A license to operate the plant was refused by government following a strong expression of public concern.

The technologies needed to modify a DNA sequence, including a germ line, of all living things is rapidly being developed. The potential for good is enormous. Equally the risks and dangers are profound. Powerful moral and ethical questions are also being raised. Genetic engineering could well follow nuclear energy down the slippery slope of disapproval.

The scientific and engineering communities themselves must address these issues, and there is a case for self-regulatory bodies. These could add to build public confidence that genuine control is at work. But statutory regulation seems the more probable outcome. The cue for such government intervention might well be in response to an accident or individual professional malpractice. A more restrictive regulatory climate imposed in the interest of public safety would be to the detriment of scientific and technological aspirations. The solution may therefore lie in our own hands to win the necessary public confidence by leading this debate rather than following public opinion in a defensive way.

Governments face an increasingly harder task in legislating wisely on these issues and simultaneously providing a stimulus to technology. Simple solutions with universal application are unlikely. Religious factors, varying historical experiences, and national concerns make bioethics a minefield. An informed government, technically literate public servants and an aware public opinion are indispensable. Without these, our ability to develop and apply new technologies will be even more difficult.

Major Government Programs

There are other ways to stimulate innovation. The French call them "les grands programmes," major national initiatives. These may fit at any point on the spectrum from basic science through defense and industrial ventures such as the Moon and Mars program, space plane, nuclear fusion, decoding the human genome, a superconducting super collider, or the Strategic Defense Initiative. Some of these projects pursue national prestige through scientific means. All require vast resources and time scales that stretch well beyond a governmental or presidential mandate. As superpower competition is replaced by cooperation, the three most powerful economic blocs—United States, Japan, and the European Community—will look for ways to avoid and defuse competitive tensions, and most likely take on programs with an international, and intercontinental character. Competition between researchers as a way of stimulating vigorous debate is one thing. Duplication of vastly expensive facilities is another. The resources required for the projects just mentioned are financial and technical investments no single country can afford alone. The obvious advantages that stem from broader international collaboration must be followed up. There are welcome signs that all the leading technological powers, including the United States, are beginning to realize this is the only logical direction to take.

The increased complexity of these international projects will bring increased tensions to the technical community and new management problems. What is needed is a mechanism to bring together the principals from each major industrial country to review and share their ideas at an early stage of gestation for these large projects. Without such a mechanism, countries are making proposals for collaboration at a late phase in the planning process and creating the impression that the collaborator is being asked to help pay but without having sufficient opportunity to contribute to the setting of goals. There is need also to set up institutional arrangements to enable collaborators to participate in the major decisions during the life of the project. The arrangements at CERN are a good example of a management system that works well. In the United States, an encouraging move is that of the Carnegie Commission on Science, Technology, and Government, which in February 1991 invited science advisers from the principal industrial nations to meet for informal discussion.

Government as the Champion of Technology

The close coupling between technology, economic performance, and quality of life encourage some to believe that government should go beyond funding basic science to also subsidize industrial product development. So-called enabling technologies are cited as examples where government intervention is justified on the grounds of international competitiveness. Debates over the desirability and extent of support for high-definition TV or the semiconductor industry are not unique to the United States. All governments aim to maximize the return on public investment in R&D, notably through technology transfer to industry.

The history of the last 30 years shows that such intervention needs to be sustained over a considerable period if it is to succeed. The Japanese ability to maintain a political and corporate consensus on technology issues has directly contributed to their success. Such continuity is less likely where there are frequent changes of government or ministerial responsibility, or where powerful lobbies can throw established policy off course because a genuine strategy is lacking. Politicians do not inherit the initiatives of their predecessors easily; they wish to put their stamp on things, generate their own initiatives. They find it difficult to accept changes of direction to fit emerging understanding of a new product or technology. My experience in industry taught me that starting new ventures is easy; stopping them is hard. In government it is virtually impossible. I have come to believe that government sponsorship of technology is fraught with difficulty. If the desired results are to be achieved, then great care is needed to develop a strategic commitment by government and industry and, at the beginning of the sponsorship, to be clear on the terms of the support and the period over which it will be provided.

In an ideal world governments would not attempt to pick either technological or industrial winners, a job for which they are ill-qualified. Instead they would sponsor high-quality academic science and provide fiscal incentives for industry to invest. As already advocated, cross-fertilization between industry and the academic community must be encouraged and strengthened, and include the use of public funds. The importance of small and medium-size companies in all economies is universally accepted, and with government support they can advance their R&D, manufacturing, and marketing skills.

INFLUENCE OF FINANCIAL INSTITUTIONS
AND ECONOMIC FACTORS

The successful commercialization of a new technology involves taking technical and financial risks. If shareholders have confidence in the ability of their management to deliver profitable new technology, they are likely to adopt a more patient attitude toward their investment. The attitude of financial institutions toward technology investment is therefore crucial. In Britain there has been much debate about the status of "patient money," the effect of mergers and acquisitions, often pan-European, and the need for demonstrably strong management. Despite the protestations of the financiers, there remains widespread belief that the long-term commitment required to pull leading-edge technologies through to commercialization is incompatible with the demand for the best quarterly corporate results and the buy and sell recommendations of the market analyst.

Yet, the structure of equity holdings varies considerably from country to country. In the United Kingdom, and to some extent in the United States, pension funds and investment trusts own much of industry, and actively trade their portfolios. In Germany and Japan, the industrial banks and conglomerates control a wide range of industry acting more as owners or active partners than third-party investors. Whatever the balance of advantage between the two approaches, the need for financial backers to understand the full importance of development work associated with technologies is undeniable.

An ethos that some attribute, possibly unfairly, to business schools such as Harvard University may also feed the tendency to short-termism. This appears to emphasize making money out of money rather than making profits from products that respond to or create a market. The creation of new and useful technologies do not fit happily with quarterly results mania and balance sheet myopia: there are no financial shortcuts to new technologies. If consistently better results are required, the answer is usually to employ competent and well-trained people, develop the best management, and build the most competitive technology.

Governments can influence this position through fiscal policies, and through intervention where they perceive market failure. But in my experience, when sound company management earns the confidence of financial institutions these same institutions both *expect* longer-term R&D investment and are *prepared* to underwrite it.

Foreign Investment

The United Kingdom is a major foreign investor. It accounted for more than 30 percent of total foreign investment in the United States at the end of 1989, more than $100 billion. Not surprisingly, the United Kingdom also strongly encourages foreign manufacturing investment in Britain. Government policy toward inward investment can stimulate job creation and economic growth. The British government believes that such benefits far outweigh the downside. There have been calls in Europe for stronger defenses against foreign investment, notably Japanese, on the ground that it constitutes an industrial Trojan horse and merely strengthens the competition facing national companies. The United Kingdom has always resisted such protectionist pressures.

In my view inward investment can be the vehicle for introducing advanced technologies, better management techniques, and enhanced market responsiveness from local suppliers: a spur to national companies, not a threat. In time, it is likely that more foreign companies would extend their commitment to include R&D activity in their portfolios as many large U.S. multinationals already do. If this becomes a mutually beneficial process, there is no reason to oppose such a trend. But it must not be used simply as a guise for exploiting local academic research labor and expertise. There must be a genuine two-way street. Current British government policy is designed to foster this.

The Globalization of Technology

The ability of governments to control technology policy has always been limited. It is almost certainly declining. The term "globalization of technology" has been coined to describe the worldwide flow of ideas and their application as processes and products. Gold used to be the currency of mercantile business. Arguably it has been supplemented or maybe even replaced by a new commodity—technology. Borders have ceased to have much significance in the exchange of technology, as the policemen of intellectual property rights will confirm. Governments are passive observers rather than active players in this process.

Globalization is most striking in industries where economy of scale is the lifeblood of competitiveness, and the semiconductor industry provides the most extreme example. With a minimum stake of $0.5 billion demanded to tool up a new generation of memory chips, it is impossible to rely on a single-country market, even one with the appetite of the United States. In such a capital-intensive and high-risk industry, the only logical solution is to go global. Although a truly global corporation has yet to be born (even IBM for all its international credentials is still at heart an all-American child), the dynamics that dictate that most high-technology industries look to the international horizon is firmly established.

Governments have to respond to that new environment. In semiconductors both the U.S. and Europe have established collaborative programs, Sematech and JESSI, to underpin their industries' competitiveness. More widely, the EC is devoting increasing funds to collaborative R&D. Possibly more important, are joint programs encouraging companies and academic centers to look for transborder research partners. The belief of companies and business executives that the European Single Market will materialize creates something of a self-fulfilling prophecy.

It has taken strenuous efforts by the EC to convince the U.S. administration and others that the Single Market does not equal the construction of fortress Europe. A similar message for its R&D programs should be stressed. This is not an attempt to shut out the rest of the world. The amounts involved are still small: the total EC R&D budget is less than 5 percent of the total research expenditures by the 12 member states. But there is a clearly rising curve. Like the United States, Europe believes that technology holds a vital key to future industrial competitiveness, and the member states of the EC are backing that belief in a legitimate fashion.

There is now a need to establish an EC-U.S. dialogue on these issues to avoid potential conflicts in the technology sector spilling over into damaging trade disputes. Individual governments will have less control over technology issues in the future, but collectively they will have increased responsibility for setting and monitoring an adequate framework for the exchange of technology.

PUBLIC UNDERSTANDING OF SCIENCE AND TECHNOLOGY

John K. Galbraith once commented, "The enemy of the market is not ideology but the engineer." Galbraith's somewhat scathing view shows that engineers and scientists need to overcome widespread distrust. There are ample grounds for believing that we are witnessing a declining public confidence in science and technology and that it is driven partly by a lack of understanding and partly by fear of the unknown. The suspicion that new and menacing technologies are going to be imposed without consent is a natural consequence. Scientists and engineers must accept a considerable share of the responsibility for such a situation, as politicians themselves are not the prime movers of public. The news media unsurprisingly highlight dramatic events, be they in space or medical advances or the failures of technology, and the tendency will always be to accentuate the negative. The scientific and engineering community must face this challenge. It cannot expect government to do the work for it. Whether it is human embryo research, the search for an AIDS vaccine, global warming, or the confidentiality of electronic data, the public has the right to expect an explanation of where science and engineering are taking society. The onus is on the technologists to make their arcane activity comprehensible to a broader community. The excuse that only Nobel Prize minds are capable of the necessary understanding is no longer acceptable in a world where individual scientific disciplines are becoming minutely fragmented.

The government role in all this is to encourage scientists and engineers to be better communicators with politicians, public servants, and the general public. Although the academies and institutions should take the lead, there is a case for

68

TECHNOLOGY AND GOVERNMENT

requiring recipients of publicly funded research grants to undertake some form of educational work, in the widest possible sense, at the conclusion of their research. The need to boost the image and credibility of engineering has never been greater especially as advanced economies face difficult demographic shifts and a decline in the numbers of science and engineering graduates following a career in their subject of study, even in Japan.

SUMMARY

Technology and the well-being of society are inseparable. The innovative character of a nation will largely decide its future and affect the quality of life for its inhabitants. But it is becoming increasingly unlikely that a single nation can expect to excel in all fields of technology. Once a technology becomes established, global forces take over. National competitiveness will depend more and more on the processes that create and apply superior technologies developed from a sound scientific foundation. Government should devote public funds to good academic science and the formation of technologies. But government commitment to developing patently superior capability must be related to those areas where industry itself shows commitment. The peer review processes within academia should perhaps take more account of this factor in judgments on the allocation of money.

Governments should encourage inward investment by companies that are participating successfully in global technologies. This provides a direct economic contribution and stimulates national industries.

Growing public unease about science and technology puts an urgent responsibility on scientists and engineers to communicate widely and in terms that can be understood, particularly by the general public, who ultimately hold sway over governments in any democratic society. The creation of a national body within the science and engineering profession to monitor and set professional standards of ethical and moral conduct might ensure the freedom to do good, useful science and push technology forward. It would also act as a confidence building measure.

There are a growing number of megaprojects in science and technology that are so costly that it is unproductive to continue, purely for reasons of national prestige, to duplicate the capital investment needed. There is a growing realization that governments must create the political conditions for a radical shift to greater international collaboration. It should be strongly encouraged.

The following quotation vividly describes the challenges we face:

There is nothing more difficult to carry out, nor more doubtful to success, nor more dangerous to handle, than to initiate a new order of things. For the reformer has enemies in all who profit by the old order and only lukewarm defenders in all those who would profit by the new order. This lukewarmness arises partly from fear of their adversaries, who have the law in their favor;

and partly from the incredulity of mankind, who do not truly believe in anything new until they have had actual experience of it.

Was the author Keynes, Friedman, Drucker? It was Machiavelli in 1513.

REFERENCE

Weinberg, A. M. 1989. Engineering in an age of anxiety. Pp. 49–59 in Engineering and Human Welfare. Washington, D.C.: National Academy of Engineering.

3
Practitioners' Perspectives

The Social Function of Engineering:
A Current Assessment

GEORGE BUGLIARELLO

Engineering affects virtually every aspect of our society and engages a substantial set of the population in carrying out engineers' plans and designs. But what is the nature of that activity? What is the role of engineering in responding to society's needs as well as in shaping them? How well does engineering carry out that role?

These questions are being asked with increasing urgency by a society that has benefited from great advances in technology, and at the same time, seen dislocations and experienced fears associated with technology—a society that has become increasingly dependent on technology, but also increasingly ambivalent about it. Often the questions about technology are confused with questions about engineering in the mind of the public despite a growing literature on the relation of technology to the rest of society.[1,2] In recent years several symposia by the National Academy of Engineering and other engineering organizations, as well as various reports and articles have addressed aspects of this relationship (Chalk, 1988; Christensen, 1987; Corcoran, 1982; National Academy of Engineering, 1970, 1974, 1980, 1988; National Research Council, 1985). In general, however, the voice of engineers in the discussion of engineering's social role has been weak, episodical, and often self-centered. The assessment of engineering's impact on society has been largely left to other disciplines. Social scientists and philosophers who have studied the technological process have achieved a considerable level of sophistication. However, because of a lack of dialogue with engineers, they too have tended to offer an idealized view of the technological process (Bijker et al., 1989; Mumford, 1934). For a nonengineering perspective on the technological process see Durbin (1978—), and Kranzberg and Davenport (1972).

The situation is quite different in the sciences. Scientists have written prolifically and in depth about the social role and impact of their activities. Nothing written by engineers is analogous to J. D. Bernal's highly ideological opus *The Social Function of Science* (1939).

SOCIAL IMPACTS OF ENGINEERING

Many engineering developments of this century with immense impacts on our lives have not been accompanied by realistic engineering views of those impacts on the social fabric or the environment. Would the societal consequences have been different if engineers had been more involved in a systematic study of engineering's complex role in society, had a working dialogue with social scientists, and had better communication with the public? For instance, could we have anticipated that the automobile would turn out to be a severe source of pollution as well as a powerful instrument of urban change, that radios in every household would catalyze the political emancipation of women, or that television would influence our values and contribute to functional illiteracy? Could we have anticipated that a broader base of affluence brought about by technology in the nations of the West would be accompanied by the rise of anomie and a drug culture among not only the poor and the disenfranchised, but also the more affluent who have in many material ways benefited the most from technology? Could we have anticipated that abundant energy for industries and homes or the invention of plastic materials would have such serious environmental consequences, and that "cleaner" technologies, such as computers, would damage the earth's ozone layer because of the use of chlorofluorocarbons in the fabrication of microchips?

The list of impacts and side effects of technology is long and growing and has contributed to society's ambivalence about technology. While it would be wrong to blame the engineer for the apparent lack of interest by large portions of society in understanding the technological process with its constraints and possibilities, engineers can do much to reduce society's ambivalence if they could overcome their own parochialism. For example, a gap that exists sometime between the perceptions of the engineers and those of the rest of society can be seen in educational technology. Engineers have tended to focus on the development of new technologies rather than the social setting—municipal bureaucracies, school systems, and homes—in which that technology is to become acceptable if it is to be successful (NAE, 1974).

Part of the difficulty engineers encounter in dealing with social issues has to do with too many definitions of engineering and the lack of agreed upon and shared tenets. The famous 1828 definition of engineering by the British Institution of Engineering—as the modification of nature (Encyclopaedia

Britannica, 1910)—was on the right track but is both too general (as other human activities also modify nature) and too specific in its subsequent detailing of those activities. The kind of definitions that later and to this day seem to have become accepted by many engineers center on the application of science to human welfare. Definitions of this kind fall wide of the mark by remaining too vague about the definition of human welfare and the role of engineering in it. They overlook the essential nature of engineering as a human activity to *modify* nature (a clear distinction between science and engineering). Furthermore, such definitions are not accompanied by a widely shared set of principles that parallel in power and simplicity the verifiable truth of the scientist, although there have been recent efforts to explore key concepts common to all engineering disciplines (see, among others, Bugliarello, 1989b).

An important point in looking at the social function of engineering is how society makes engineering possible. A complex feedback situation emerges. The artifacts extend the power and reach of society and the individual. Society, in turn, through its organizations and demands, makes possible the development of complex artifacts and stimulates their constant technical evolution and diffusion. Today, to talk about the impact of engineering on society is meaningless without also talking about the impact of society on engineering, and how it shapes the role of engineering. The complexity of the interactions between society and engineering is at the root of unrealistic expectations about engineering, as social entities are often inadequately organized to develop and use engineering effectively. It is also at the root of the frustration of engineers unable to bring their capabilities to bear on the solution of social problems or the effective organization of the engineering enterprise.

SOCIOLOGY AND EDUCATION OF ENGINEERS

To understand how engineering responds to the needs of society, we must examine its social structure and its function. Most people who study engineering in the United States have higher mathematics skills than verbal and social ones. This limits their involvement in politics and their success in communicating with the rest of society. Society, in turn, often views the engineer as a narrow, conservative, numbers-driven person, insensitive to subtle societal issues.

The systematic study of sociotechnical problems is rarely included in the engineering curricula as an important sphere of engineering activity. The curriculum focuses on man-made artifacts to the exclusion, except for specialized cases, of biological systems and organisms. This narrow focus has kept engineering away from not only a rich source of inspiration for specific technical feats and lessons offered by systems of great subtlety and complexity, but also a deeper understanding of environmental change.

Most high school students today do not view an engineering education as a path to success and prestige worthy of the sacrifices of a rigorous curriculum.

It is rarely chosen by the offspring of the well-to-do and the socially prominent. Even bright young engineering students, upon graduation, switch to careers in business management, law, and medicine. On the other hand, engineering continues to be a powerful instrument for social mobility and advancement for immigrants and the poor. This situation accentuates the perceived social gap between engineers and other professions in society. It is further reinforced by massive layoffs in defense industries and practices in the construction business that treat engineers more as commodities than as professionals (Jacobs, 1989).

In different societies engineering provides most of the same artifacts: shelter, energy and communications, manufacturing, water supply, extraction and use of resources, and disposal of waste. There are societies where engineers carry out broader functions by virtue of the position they hold. In several European and developing countries, they head state organizations and major industry conglomerates, participate in government, and enjoy high social prestige. By contrast, engineers in the United States are absent from major positions of societal leadership, and only a handful serve in Congress, as governors, or at the cabinet level.

In the United States the number of engineers per capita is roughly half that of Japan. Coupled with layoffs, this is an indicator of how seriously "underengineered" the United States is. The situation needs to be addressed not only in terms of supply and demand of engineers, but also in terms of the basic structure and direction of the country. In so doing, we must be mindful of historical precedents of decline—like Rome of the third and fourth centuries or the Ottoman Empire of the seventeenth century—which some historians believe started with a decline of interest in technology (de Camp, 1975; Kinross, 1977).

The profession is, in a sense, handicapped in terms of serving society in a broader way by a "pecking order" that prizes activities connected with the design of tangible artifacts above the challenges of manufacturing, operations, and maintenance. We need more national and transnational studies of the engineer's origins, careers, institutions, rewards, means of communicating, and so forth to gain a broader understanding of the engineer's role and effectiveness in society. Some of these factors are now receiving attention in the literature out of a concern about engineering ethics (Layton, 1986; Unger, 1982).

Social Responsibility

The burning question for engineering in extending the outreach of society is: What is responsible outreach? The answer is perhaps best given in evolutionary terms. Man-made artifacts, albeit extensions of our body, have not evolved through the gradual process that has shaped man and other biological species. Thus, we constantly face the question of whether the technology we develop enhances the long-range survival of our species. Because assessing how well engineering carries out its social function lacks the ultimate test of the crucible of evolution, we need to define what we mean by the "social responsibility" of engineering. In the following paragraphs, I offer five guiding principles, some of which are already deeply embedded in the conscience of engineers.

Uphold the dignity of man. The dignity of man is an imponderable in terms of a clear evolutionary meaning. However, it is a fundamental value of our society that never should be violated by an engineering design. This happens when the design or operation of a technological product (a building, a machine, a procedure) fails to recognize the importance of individuality, privacy, diversity, and aesthetics and is based on a stereotyped view of a human being.

Avoid dangerous or uncontrolled side effects and by-products. The challenge to engineering is how to fulfill its social purpose in ways that either control side effects and by-products or make them more easily foreseeable. This demands a rigorous preliminary examination of how to solve a problem and achieve a given social purpose. The problem is complicated beyond measure by the multitude of pressures leading to the development of a design or a technology—be they political, economic, popular, or intrinsically technological. These pressures can lead to unwise outcomes beyond the ability of engineering to solve, for example, the deferral of municipal maintenance due to constrained budgets or the abandonment of nuclear power plants in some Western countries.

Make provisions for consequence when technology fails. The importance of making provisions for the consequences of failure is self-evident, especially in those systems that are complex, pervasive, and place us at great risk if they fail. A simple example is the failure of an air-conditioning system in a closed ventilation system, as occurred tragically in 1990 at Mecca, with the loss of over a thousand lives (*Newsweek*, 1990). A more complex example is the space shuttle. Because it is the sole vehicle for a multitude of space tasks, any of its failures sets back our position in space.

Avoid buttressing social systems that perform poorly and should be replaced. This runs much against the grain of most engineers. Thanks to a multitude of technological and engineering fixes (Weinberg, 1966), our society often avoids rethinking fundamental social issues and organization. However, short-run technological fixes can put us at much greater risk in the long term. In the case of energy, for instance, technological or commercial fixes cannot mask the need to rethink globally the impact of consumerism and the interrelationship of energy, environment, and economic development.

Participate in formulating the "why" of technology. At present the engineering profession is poorly equipped to do so both in this country and elsewhere. Few engineers, for instance, have been involved in developing a philosophy of technology—as distinct from that of science—and in teaching the subject in engineering schools.[3] Yet, John Dewey saw the problems of philosophy and those of technology as inseparable at the beginning of this century (Hickman, 1990). This separation of engineering and philosophy affects our entire society. Engineers, in shaping our future, need to be guided by a clearer sense of the meaning and evolutionary role of technology. The great social challenges we face require a rethinking of the human-artifact-society interrelationship and the options it offers us to carry out a growing number of social functions using quasi-intelligent artifacts to instruct, manufacture, inspect, control, and so on. We also need to think through the implications of a shift from energy to information (for example, for issues relating to urban planning and the environment), and the possibilities of "hyperintelligence"—the enhancement of the social intelligence of our species through the interaction of humans and global computer networks (Bugliarello, 1984a, 1988, 1989a).

Social Purpose

How well does engineering fulfill it social purpose? This apparently simple question presents several problems.

Which social group are engineers trying to satisfy? Is it a family, a tribe, a company, a municipality, a nation, or a supernational global entity? It is clear that different groups have different technological needs and expectations, and that if engineering satisfies some groups, it may not satisfy others.

What about the needs of the engineers themselves as a social group? A technology that does not respond to the interests of other social groups but serves exclusively its own purposes evinces concerns about autonomous or runaway technology (Winner, 1977). While it is possible to envision such an occurrence for a technological system, the likelihood of runaway engineering is generally remote, if only because engineers, as a cog in the technological system, are unable to be autonomous and "run away" with their designs (Florman, 1987; Veblen, 1921) and are most often subservient to contingent pressures of a social group.

The term *satisfaction* lacks a rigorous definition necessary to describe an engineering response to a particular social need. The dimensions of a social group are a particularly important factor. In the case of small social groups resources are generally too limited to develop anything but the simplest technologies. Even the wealthiest of families today could not, even if they wished it, mount a manned exploration of space. Hence, small social groups, as well as large, unorganized populations, can only use today's technologies, not create them. With this comes the associated danger of alienation from technology or of resentment spurred by limited participation and ignorance. At a national and global scale, there is a similar lack of powerful supranational organizations to mobilize and control technological resources. Hence, the danger of global environmental damage continues. Today, intermediate-size organizations—corporations and governmental bodies—are most effective in mobilizing technology in response to their needs.

An important determinant of how well engineering satisfies its social purpose is the breadth of engineering. Engineering today continues overwhelmingly to focus on inanimate artifacts or machines, just as engineering school curricula worldwide continue to bypass sociotechnological integrations like the biomachine—the ever-growing interaction and interpenetration of biological and machine systems.[4] This lopsided orientation grew out of obvious historical origins that have had major consequences for society. The factory environment so single-mindedly rationalized by the engineer F. W. Taylor overlooked the effective integration of the worker—the biological unit—and the machine in the production process. This is so almost everywhere in the world, with the notable exception of Japan, where a different social ethos has produced a more effective integration. At the opposite end of the spectrum is the anomie of the worker in Eastern Europe.

Social Needs

The various needs of social groups that engineering and technology may be expected to satisfy are educational (mentioned earlier), economic, environmental, health, public service, spiritual, and defense. It is important to underscore that, in seeking to satisfy these needs, engineering cannot be shackled to short-range and narrow technical applications. It must be allowed to explore new extensions of our biological capability.

The recurrent conflict between advocates of independent and targeted research is an example and an inevitable result of the tension between short- and long-range needs. If pushed to the extreme, however, such conflicts may cross the boundary between what is socially useful and what is out of control.

At the intellectual core of the sluggish and somewhat myopic response of U.S. engineering to environmental needs is the lack of basic environmental principles embedded by education in the consciousness of all engineers. A key principle, for instance, is recognition that any artifact—any alteration of nature—inevitably has an effect on the environment, and particularly on the humans and other living organisms in it. Another key principle is the requirement, as an essential component of the design process, to address those impacts to the satisfaction not only of the engineer and the engineer's employer but also of the general public.

The health care system has absorbed an ever-greater portion of our gross national product, regardless of the state of our economic prosperity. At the same time, it has priced itself outside the financial reach of almost 40 million Americans. Technology has abetted the situation, not only by favoring the higher-cost, high-repair segment of the system, but also by not addressing the structure of the system (Bugliarello, 1984b). Similarly the problem of hunger remains endemic in many parts of the globe despite advances in agricultural technology. Even when production is high, in many countries grain supplies rot for lack of effective storage and distribution systems.

The pattern of technology repeats itself in the way we address problems of infrastructure, education, and poverty, or the problems of the metropolitan areas that now are home to more than 75 percent of our population. For instance, the problem of housing for the poor and homeless in many developing countries as well as in the United States persists despite our knowledge of building techniques and materials. We need to organize a system of production, distribution, self-help, and education to put that knowledge to work for the dispossessed.

Technology and science working in concert have demythologized many social and cultural beliefs and left a spiritual no-man's-land. Paradoxically, the very success envisioned by eighteenth-century encyclopedists—man's conquest of nature—has confused our society, sweeping away the certainties of the past and leaving society in need of guidance and new orthodoxies. Cars, airplanes, telecommunications, fast foods, and contraceptives have brought about a drastic restructuring of social customs and processes and a jadedness about technological advances. It may be argued that engineers need to question their cultural responsibility to society as they contribute to its change. This effort must begin in the universities. The task is particularly daunting for the United States, with its thin line of 20,000 engineering teachers of growing disparity in cultural backgrounds.

The social role of engineering cannot overlook military engineering—the activity from which modern engineering is derived—as one of the most controversial facets of that role (Mitcham and Siekevitz, 1989). Although military engineering is not viewed by everyone as fulfilling a useful social role, it is crucial for the survival and success of a society. The importance of that social role to the long-term future of a society can be a matter of judgment—and hence open to controversy in the context of a hoped for reduction of military confrontations.

The specialist's role of the engineer seems to prevail today—a retreat from the situation in the last century and earlier in this century, when engineers like Herbert Spencer or Vilfredo Pareto took broader views of society and developed new economic, social or political ideas. The dominance, particularly in our country, of the purely technical over the broader role of engineering can be attributed primarily to the sociological characteristics of engineering and to the inadequacy of engineering education in preparing students for broad social leadership. This is so in spite of the fact that the earliest U.S. technological universities hark back conceptually to the model of the French "Ecole Poly-technique," with its purpose of producing technically prepared leaders. Indeed, it may be argued that the rigorous professionalization of engineering has been achieved in our country at the expense of preparation for broader leadership roles.

To reiterate, any attempt to rate the current performance of engineering in the satisfaction of social needs must take into account at least three factors: (1)

the fundamental difficulty that engineers encounter in addressing major social problems given a lack of an adequate sociotechnological preparation, (2) the propensity of engineers to find technological fixes for existing social systems rather than to develop and use technological innovations to accomplish needed social change, and (3) the ensuing limited or simplistic views of the social role of engineering.

LESSONS LEARNED

A current assessment of the purposes, roles, and aspirations for engineering and society suggest some pathways to more effective partnerships:

1.   When social systems and technology have been able to complement each other, engineering has been immensely effective in improving human life by augmenting agricultural production, building infrastructure, producing jobs, improving public health, etc.

2.   Engineering can best carry out its social purpose when it is involved in the formulation of the response to a social need, rather than just being called to provide a quick technological fix. Often, a technological fix is in the long run counterproductive. The Sahel economy was devastated, at least in part, when local populations were persuaded to abandon animal power for motor-driven vehicles and pumps—only to find them immobilized when the OPEC cartel made fuel inaccessibly expensive.

3.   Society and technology—and hence engineering—fail, often spectacularly, when the social system is hostile or unwilling to modify itself to allow technology to operate under the best conditions for producing beneficial results. Nowhere is this more obvious than in societal failures to alleviate problems of hunger, illiteracy, and health care.

4.   Engineering can respond to a societal purpose in the measure that such a purpose is well articulated. However, even if well articulated, the social purpose may be detrimental to society and to humankind in general. Engineering, as a force of society, can and should intervene in correcting a social purpose it perceives as detrimental. Historically, this has been very difficult to do. Engineering has tended to respond to the social system in which it is embedded: in market economies it has made unbridled consumerism possible, and in authoritarian regimes it has provided the technological means that reinforce the regimes' power.

5.   Whether, even within the framework of existing socioeconomic systems, engineering has served well the social purpose of those systems is a complex question. Engineering, to the extent it has influence on the process, may have failed in this more limited context if a market economy produces consumer goods that do not stand up well to competition or pollute dangerously, or if a nonmarket economy produces artifacts that are shoddy, such as much of public housing in Eastern Europe.

WHAT IS PAST IS PROLOGUE:
THE AMERICAN EXPERIENCE

In the past 25 years, several major trends have emerged that magnify the social impact of engineering and the challenge to engineering to address pivotal social issues. These trends are too well known and documented to be further underscored here: the sharpening of engineering prowess in the creation of artifacts; the broadening of the social needs that engineering is called to address; geopolitical and economic shifts that are placing new demands on engineering; the coming to the fore of a series of issues of wide societal impact—such as the environment—that stem at least in part from engineering and technology themselves and demand urgent attention.

To focus more specifically on the situation today in the United States, it is clear that engineering continues to perform effectively the task of generating new technological ideas. However, with broad exceptions—such as aerospace, the chemical and pharmaceutical industries, biotechnology, computers, and telecommunications—U.S. technology has not been very successful in maintaining a strong position against capable and aggressive commercial competitors from abroad (NAE, 1988). This failing brings substantial job losses in manufacturing and raises the fear that the United States, despite its prowess in military technology, is becoming a second-class technological power. It also weakens the nation's ability to respond to the cries for help and to the hopes of the poor and the disenfranchised throughout the world.

Engineering has contributed to this situation by its failure to emphasize manufacturing and production in formal engineering education and in the system of professional recognition. That emphasis is being developed, laboriously, only now. U.S. engineering has been slow also in responding to the immense challenges of globalization, and of the environment. The globally spreading networks of designers, factories, research laboratories, data banks, and sales and marketing operations require a new conception of how the engineering enterprise is organized and of how engineers are trained and certified. For instance, the likely development of international teams working around the clock on the same design from different locations will lead to the creation of new engineering specialties. Globalization also means extreme competitiveness, with greater potential instabilities for engineering enterprises and the employment of engineers. But the greatest challenge that globalization presents engineers and engineering education is how to increase throughout the world the rate of technological, economic, and social progress through the creation of new and more adaptable technologies and better sociotechnical integration.

Furthermore, U.S. engineering has not participated to any major extent in the development of strategies for the reform of the health care and education systems as two key service activities that together absorb well over 15 percent of our GNP. In the case of health care, engineering has produced a host of innovative technologies, which, applied within the framework of an obsolete system, have added greatly to cost, without correspondingly improving national mortality statistics and access to health care (Bugliarello, 1984b). Similarly, although engineering provides education with powerful tools, it has little impact on an education system that remains largely an artisan enterprise, incapable of reorganizing itself to take full advantage of the great potential offered by systems, information, and telecommunications technology.

Engineering also has been absent from the attack on some of the most vexing problems of urban areas. Poverty, drugs, and alienation are all interconnected sociotechnological problems of our cities, with their deteriorating infrastructure and the loss of easily accessible jobs in manufacturing.

A further example of engineering acquiescence in the subordination of technological possibilities and common sense is the anarchical situation in the United States concerning telecommunications. The current absence of a plan for the transition to fiber optics may deny the United States, to the advantage of its competitors abroad, the possibility of developing integrated new technologies for the largest telecommunications system and the biggest computer market in the world (Keyworth and Abell, 1990).

Contributing to the difficulty of U.S. engineering in addressing major social problems is the limited participation of women and African-American, Hispanic, and Native American minorities in the engineering enterprise. These groups are more squarely in the middle of most of those problems, and bring to engineering an enhanced sensitivity and urgency, as well as broader societal support. Much is being done today to attract women and underrepresented minorities to engineering, but it must be remembered that, as late as the early 1970s, there was a fairly strong opposition among engineers themselves to the recruitment of women (Bugliarello et al., 1972). The recruitment of minorities at that time was also limited, as it continues to be today despite major efforts over the intervening 20 years.

It has been said that this is the first generation in the history of the United States that has lost the hope of being better off than the previous generation. That view is too sweeping. Consider, for example, the immigrants and the great progress made on improving the economic conditions of minorities. However, to the extent that there is a perception of loss, much of it is undoubtedly associated with the weakening of our industrial competitiveness and with the sense that American technology, once believed to be the foundation of our success as a society, is not necessarily the harbinger of an ever-better future for Americans. Hence, regaining industrial competitiveness in manufacturing and addressing crucial social problems are challenges that American engineering must address if it is to help instill in our society a greater sense of optimism about the future.

ENGINEERING AT A CROSSROADS

Operating at the core of the technological process, engineering has succeeded in extending by orders of magnitude several of our biological capabilities. Many achievements of the modern world, from megacities to factories to artificial organs to the human presence in space, bear witness to the enormous technical prowess and social impact of engineering. Yet, engineering has exerted little purposeful influence in shaping the social systems that have been fostered and enriched by it.

Today engineering has an unprecedented opportunity to exercise leadership in showing how technology can offer the means for creating a better world out of the ashes of collapsing or obsolete political and economic systems. The involvement of the engineer as a committed, scientifically knowledgeable problem solver and modifier of nature is our best hope for solving the problems of poverty and hunger, for eliminating the atavistic recourse to war and violence, and for addressing the environmental problem. It is also our best hope for addressing a myriad of other challenges, from natural disasters to drugs, and from water supply to a better space policy.

There is no chance, however, for these hopes to become a reality unless the technical means created by engineering are integrated toward a common global purpose. If our society is to mount an intelligent all-out attack on some of its most enduring and elusive problems, stronger engineering and technological influence and a better sense of technological possibilities are needed in the planning and execution of social interventions worldwide, both public and private.

For instance, our cities offer vast opportunities for engineering in restoring housing stocks and municipal services, and in forming new urban job-creating technologies and enterprises (Bugliarello, 1991; Mayor's Commission, 1989). However, those opportunities cannot be realized as long as engineers continue to occupy subordinate positions in municipal hierarchies and are not prepared to take the lead in drawing bold plans to address these issues—city by city, town by town. Engineers must fight major battles with bureaucracies, unions, and obsolete political jurisdictions (such as in the functionally inseparable tristate area of metropolitan New York) to make the possible real.

Thus, the great challenge to engineering, worldwide, is whether it can demonstrate the promise of an enlightened technology by placing society's more immediate needs in a broader context. Our choice, as engineers, is clear: Are we willing to ensure that the new technologies are placed in a context that affords the maximum utility to society? Or are we satisfied with confining our task to the creation of technologies that make change possible? Will we broaden our social role and take the lead in developing more integrated sociotechnological approaches to society's problems? Or will we continue to play a specialist's role without participating in the broader decisions about technology in the future of our society?

If engineers are to play a more decisive and enlightened social role, the engineering community must be willing to act on a number of issues:

- Work more closely with leaders of business and government to develop a sense of engineering and technology as one of the essential components of their preparation.
- Engage more actively in the political dialogue and in the definition of sociotechnological problems.
- Increase attention to complex sociotechnological problems, such as poverty or education, and propose new institutions, such as "technological magistratures" with combined technical and legislative power, to address complex sociotechnological problems.
- Reshape engineering education to serve society as well as the engineering community.
- Foster the involvement of engineers in cultivating the philosophy of technology, the rational and moral underpinnings of the modification of nature and the creation of artifacts.

At the outset of this paper, I raised several questions about engineering: its nature as a social activity, its role in responding to societal needs and shaping them, and its effectiveness in doing so, particularly in the United States. To conclude, engineering has performed extraordinarily well in responding to technical challenges but has shied away from the vigorous pursuit of complex sociotechnological issues. This is surely the Achilles heel of U.S. engineering. If unaddressed, this weakness will do a disservice to society by confining engineers to a mainly technical role in the engine compartments of society. Until engineering is prepared to assume greater leadership, it will remain a most honorable and skillful profession, but it will renounce its legitimate role as a splendid manifestation of humankind's will to control its destiny.

ACKNOWLEDGMENTS

I would like to gratefully acknowledge Professor Walter Rosenblith of the Massachusetts Institute of Technology and Hedy Sladovich of the National Academy of Engineering for their painstaking review and editing of this paper; Professor Steven Goldman of Lehigh University, for having kindly rushed to me the manuscript of his forthcoming entry on Engineering Education in the Encyclopedia of Higher Education; Professor Carl Mitcham of Pennsylvania State University for his bibliographical guidance; Dr. Joseph Jacobs of Jacobs Engineering for his views on the issue of engineering services tending to be treated as a commodity; Professor George Schillinger of Polytechnic University for his penetrating comments; and the Library of Polytechnic University and Rose Emma of my staff for their generous help.

NOTES

1. *Engineering* is the core activity of technology performed by a social group—the engineers—within the technological enterprise; it involves the design, construction, and operation of artifacts (as defined below). The term *engineering* is used to denote the complex of activities in which engineers engage, and of knowledge and institutions that form, organize, guide, and support engineers. The methodology of engineering is a general problem-solving one that resorts heavily to the sciences and mathematics and can have uses beyond engineering. The modifications of nature by engineers take many forms in response to social needs.
   Technology is a social activity. It responds to the needs of a social group to modify nature for the group's purposes. Technology is carried out by a subset (which includes engineers) of that social group; its products and by-products (artifacts) affect that social group, and society in general.
   Artifacts—at least the wanted ones—are designed to enhance extracorporeally the capabilities of biological organisms, and in so doing enhance society. It is useful to formally define an artifact as any man-made, or, more generally, any biologically made modification of nature. Roads, buildings, mechanical machines, microchips, are obvious artifacts, as they modify nature and are not a product of a natural ecological process. A computer program and a musical score are also artifacts. Today's changing atmosphere can be viewed as an artifact to the extent that it is affected by emissions from factories, automobiles, agriculture, and other human artifacts and activities. Medical intervention in the course of a natural process we call disease is also an artifact, making it akin to engineering in its science-influenced endeavor to modify nature.
   Art, like engineering, enhances society through the creation of artifacts that at times come close to engineering, as in architecture and a number of contemporary artwork involving electronics, optics (e.g., motion pictures), new materials (e.g., acrylic painting), and new system concepts (e.g., feedback art) (Bugliarello, 1984c).
2. See journals such as *Bulletin of Science, Technology and Society* (1980—), *Technology in Society* (1978—).
3. For examples of joint attempts by engineers, philosophers, and historians to address issues of the philosophy and history of technology, see Bugliarello and Doner, eds. (1979); a recent, albeit controversial, study of the philosophy of technology by Agassi (1985); and a comprehensive year-by-year bibliographical review of the philosophy of technology by C. Mitcham in Durbin (1978—).
4. Exceptions to this are the specialized fields of bioengineering and biochemical engineering and certain aspects of chemical engineering.

REFERENCES

Agassi, J. 1985. Technology—Philosophical and Social Aspects. Dordrecht: Reidel.
Bernal, J. D. 1939. The Social Function of Science. New York: Macmillan.
Bijker, W., T. Hughes, and T. Pinch, eds. 1989. The Social Construction of Techno-
logical Systems. Cambridge, Mass.: MIT Press.

Bugliarello, G., V. Cardwell, D. Salembier, and W. White, eds. 1972. Women in Engineering. Chicago: University of Illinois at Chicago Circle.

Bugliarello, G. 1984a. Hyperintelligence. The Futurist (December):6–11.

Bugliarello, G. 1984b. Health care costs: Technology to the rescue? IEEE Spectrum (June):97–100.

Bugliarello, G. 1984c. Tecnologia. Enciclopedia del Novecento. Roma: Istituto della Enciclopedia Italiana. VII:382–414. Translated and edited as The Intelligent Layman's Guide to Technology. 1987. Brooklyn, N.Y.: Polytechnic Press.

Bugliarello, G. 1988. Toward hyperintelligence. Knowledge: Creation, Diffusion, Utilization 10(1):67–89.

Bugliarello, G. 1989a. Technology and the environment. Pp. 383–402 in Changing the Global Environment, Botkin, Caswell, Estes, and Orio, eds. San Diego, Calif.: Academic Press.

Bugliarello, G. 1991. Technology and the city. Paper presented at Conference on Megacities, United Nations University, Tokyo.

Bugliarello, G. 1989b. Physical and Information Sciences and Engineering. Report of the Project 2061 Phase 1, Physical and Information Sciences and Engineering Panel, Washington, D.C.: American Association for the Advancement of Science.

Bugliarello, G., and D. Doner, eds. 1979. The History and Philosophy of Technology. Urbana, Ill.: University of Illinois Press.

Chalk, R., ed. 1988. Science, Technology, and Society—Emerging Relationships. Washington, D.C.: American Association for the Advancement of Science.

Christensen, D., ed. 1987. Engineering Excellence—Cultural and Organizational Factors. New York: IEEE Press.

Corcoran, W. 1982. Engineering Education: Aims and Goals for the Eighties. Washington, D.C.: Accreditation Board for Engineering and Technology, Inc.

de Camp, L. 1975. The Ancient Engineers. New York: Ballantine.

Durbin, P., ed. 1978—. Research in Philosophy and Technology. Greenwich, Conn.: Jai Press.

Encyclopaedia Britannica. 1910. Eleventh Edition, Vol. IX. New York: The Encyclopaedia Britannica Co.

Florman, S. 1987. The Civilized Engineer. New York: St. Martin's Press.

Hickman, L. 1990. John Dewey's Pragmatic Technology. Bloomington, Ind.: Indiana University Press.

Jacobs, J. 1989. Engineering and construction: An industry in transition. Chemical Engineering Progress June:26–29.

Keyworth, G., II, and B. Abell. 1990. Competitiveness and Telecommunications. America's Economic Future: The House-to-House Digital Fiber Optic Network. Indianapolis, Ind.: Hudson Institute.

Kinross, Lord. 1977. The Ottoman Centuries: The Rise and Fall of the Turkish Empire. New York: Morrow.

Kranzberg, M., and W. H. Davenport. 1972. Technology and Culture—An Anthology. New York: Meridian.

Layton, E., Jr. 1986. The Revolt of the Engineers: Social Responsibility and the American Engineering Profession. Baltimore: Johns Hopkins University Press.

Mayor's Commission for Science & Technology. 1989. Science & Technology in New York City for the 21st Century (G. Bugliarello, committee chairman). Brooklyn, N.Y.: Polytechnic Press.

Mitcham, C., and P. Siekevitz, eds. 1989. Ethical Issues Associated with Scientific and Technological Research for the Military. Annals of the New York Academy of Sciences 577. New York: New York Academy of Sciences.

Mumford, L. 1934. Technics and Civilization. New York: Harcourt, Brace and World.
National Academy of Engineering. 1970. Engineering for the Benefit of Mankind (H. F. Barr, committee chairman). Washington, D.C.: National Academy of Engineering.
National Academy of Engineering. 1974. Issues and Public Policies in Educational Technology: To Realize the Promise. Commission on Education, Advisory Committee on Issues in Educational Technology (G. Bugliarello, committee chairman). Lexington, Mass.: Lexington Books, D.C. Heath & Company.
National Academy of Engineering. 1980. Issues in Engineering: A Framework for Analysis (B. Boley, committee chairman). Washington, D.C.: National Academy of Engineering.
National Academy of Engineering. 1988. The Technological Dimensions of International Competitiveness. Report of the Committee on Technology Issues That Impact International Competitiveness. Washington, D.C.: National Academy of Engineering.
National Academy of Engineering. 1989. Engineering and the Advancement of Human Welfare: Ten Outstanding Achievements 1964-1989. Washington, D.C.: National Academy of Engineering.
National Research Council. 1985. Engineering in Society (George S. Ansell, panel chairman). Washington, D.C.: National Academy Press.
Newsweek. 1990. Death in the Holy City. July 16, p. 38.
Unger, S. 1982. Controlling Technology: Ethics and the Responsible Engineer. New York: Holt, Rinehart and Winston.
Veblen, T. 1921. Engineers and the Price System. New York: Viking.
Weinberg, A. M. 1966. Can technology replace social engineering? Bulletin of the Atomic Scientists 22(10):4–8.
Winner, L. 1977. Autonomous Technology: Technics-Out-of-Control as a Theme in Political Thought. Cambridge, Mass.: MIT Press.

Pondering the Unpredictability of the Sociotechnical System

ROBERT W. LUCKY

How is society influenced by technology? How in turn does society shape technology? These are complex philosophical questions that we seldom consider or debate. As individual engineers we seem powerless before the omnipotence of society as a whole. Our livelihoods appear to be determined by the fickle whims of government and market forces—forces that signal to the engineering community the needs of society in ways that are in the short term tenuous and difficult to read, while in the long term compelling. The engineer tries to swim in these forces like a minnow in a school, following the fashions of the day. Those that swim against the tide are soon forgotten. In the day-to-day solving of problems that we engineers face, we seldom have the opportunity to stand on the shore and observe the flow of this external tide. Yet who sets these tidal forces in place? In some mysterious way, we all do.

MODEL FOR SOCIAL NEEDS

As engineers we seek to understand systems by constructing simplified models. I confess that I have such a model for the changing societal needs. It is not a model that many people will be happy with, but it is one that captivates me, and expresses the deep frustrations and impotencies that are endemic in our society. I hesitate to raise it before the august body of my professional peers, but it is based on the old-fashioned Ouija board.

Perhaps they have since passed from fashion, but I remember the childhood curiosity of using a Ouija board to predict the future. This is a board with letters of the alphabet and "yes" and "no" inscribed, together with a movable pointer that rides on the board similar in shape and feel to the computer mouse of today. All the players join their hands upon the pointer, and someone asks the Ouija board a question. With a slight trembling hesitation and a few false starts the pointer begins to move from place to place on the board, its passage traversing certain inscribed letters that are given great significance by all present as an other-world answer to the question posed.

The Ouija board contained great magic. Why did the pointer move at all, and why did it point where it pointed? As a budding scientist, I rejected the notion of supernatural intervention. Since I was not consciously steering the pointer myself, someone else must have been dictating its motion. I was skeptical when I always found that other people felt exactly the same way. They were not in control; someone else was. In some mysterious way the Ouija pointer expresses the common will of the participants in directions that are often surprising to all.

I have often felt exactly the same way about how social concerns shape the engineering environment. The nation—and more and more, the world—has its collective hands on a pointer that moves unbidden past squares denoting fashion, style, trends, needs, wishes, and such. Unlike the parlor Ouija board, however, the board here is so large that individual players are unable to see the movements of the pointer directly. Instead, there are privileged spectators representing the media who report on their interpretation of what they see. We get these media interpretations continuously during the game, and they seem to influence the tenuous, erratic course of the all-knowing pointer. But none of us determines that course; only the fragile, unconscious collusion of this or that segment of society does. It is perhaps an instance of chaos.

Our predictions for the future take the form of judging the current movements of the pointer. Someone says that the pointer is moving in a northeast direction. No one dares to suggest that the pointer *will* move in a northeast direction. Like yesterday's stock market results, the needs and desires of society seem calculable only in retrospect. Looking back, we say that because of this trend or that discovery, we should have known that such and such would happen. In addition to expressing the common will of society, the pointer seems to be affected by random fluctuations caused by perturbations external to the participants. Partly this random influence reflects a low-level, societal noise of a thermal nature whose occasional fluctuations drive the pointer into unexpected states, but partly also the randomness has as its origin the sporadic impulses of cataclysmic events. These happenings are like lightening bolts on the Ouija board of societal behavior.

Recent history highlights many examples of cataclysmic events that change the taste and wishes of society. Three Mile Island teaches us about meltdown, and we turn away from nuclear power. OPEC fixes petroleum allocations, and we discover the attraction of fuel efficiency. The *Exxon Valdez* runs aground in Alaska, a chemical plant in Bhopal spews toxic fumes, and one winter morning we see on television the breaking up of the Berlin wall—cataclysmic events all. Each event had many smaller, predictive antecedents, but in each case the occurrence of the event itself rivets people's attention, and the collective will triggered by the broadcast news moves the pointer determinedly in a new direction.

As I look to the future, I do not expect the basic character of this model to change. However, there will be changes in the playing of the game. For example, the board has been globalized. More significant players huddle around the table and influence directions. Moreover, the time constants associated with pointer movements are becoming shorter. The increasing global communications infrastructure has eliminated the information float. All of the players get faster feedback on the shape that societal needs is taking at any given instant. Governments, businesses, and the media take daily polls to tell us what we are thinking. The financial communities vibrate ever faster with the slightest news. Indeed, those of us who have studied control theory wonder about the stability of the system as the gain is turned ever higher.

Amidst this complex world of human drama, the domain of engineering seems clear and simple. We bring capabilities to society—tools that can augment man's mind and muscle, that can lead to better communications, entertainment, education, transportation, and the things that make life pleasant, productive, meaningful, and enjoyable. But the technological products are only tools in themselves; they must be accepted and used by society for its betterment. Where engineers often see simple solutions, society sees underlying difficulty.

Society is wary of technology and distrustful of seemingly naive techno-logical solutions to societal problems. Technologists are often forgetful of this widely held aversion. I was made painfully aware of this during an appearance as a guest on a television talk show devoted to the future. After speaking glibly about a future made more pleasant by robots, high-definition television, enhanced entertainment and education, and the like, I was roundly criticized by the other guests, who insisted the future is bleak. The environmentalist on the television show was strident in his recitation of statistics on pollution. The educator spoke of the decline in literacy. The economist talked about global starvation, and the cop-turned-television-producer sitting beside me on the sofa warned of the inevitability of drugs and crime. The gun inside his pants leg pushed against me and seemed to lend a physical reality to his worldly insight. Everyone agreed that cities were decaying. Forlornly, I held to my optimistic view that now is a much better time to live than a century ago, thanks largely to technology; I expected the future to be even better. They looked at me with scorn. What does a technologist know about such things?

Silicon Dreams (1989, St. Martin's Press), a book I recently wrote about information technology, suffered a critical review for a similar reason. "Lucky displays complete optimism about technology and its ineluctable contribution to progress and the well-being of all people," the reviewer complained. "An optimistic attitude like this is expected from engineers, who regularly tackle seemingly impossible tasks, and it no doubt makes technological advance possible." This reviewer holds little enthusiasm for "technological advance." Many people share his views, I am sure.

Although the review contains an underlying antipathy to the engineering attitude, there is an element of truth to the logic. Engineers are often unreasonably optimistic about the application of technology, but as a consequence we make progress possible where none is expected. Unaware that cities are a hopeless cause, we design urban transportation systems like BART [Bay Area Rapid Transit] or the Washington Metro that transform the urban environment. Oblivious to the hopelessness of the educational crisis, we design and build technological aids to education. Drugs may overwhelm the urban population, but we work toward increasing industrial productivity and enhancing leisure time enjoyment. Yes, we are often naive about social imperatives, but our single-mindedness can also be a positive attribute.

HOW SOCIETY APPLIES TECHNOLOGY

When I look at the history of my own field—telecommunications—I can only shake my head in frustration at the inability of technology to either follow or lead society. It reminds me of two clumsy people trying to dance, each attempting to lead with the wrong foot. Let me cite four examples—the Picturephone® , home information systems, facsimile, and cellular telephony. The first two were technologically driven market failures, while the last two were unanticipated market successes.

The Picturephone

The Picturephone® was a celebrated development of the Bell System in the late 1960s. It was a personal irony for me that when I took a course in "managing innovation" during this period, the development of Picturephone was used as a case study of a "perfect" technological development. It met schedule and cost objectives while overcoming significant technical obstacles. Unfortunately, it was soon to be discovered, there was more to life than successful technology.

The Picturephone® was introduced as a product in 1971, primarily in Chicago, with a monthly price of about $125. Market studies had, of course, predicted its acceptance and growth. The mathematical model of the predicted market growth was similar to that of a contagious disease—you did not want to be the first to get one, but after a certain number of your friends got one, you would be likely to jump on the bandwagon. Thus it was predicted that the market would start slowly and then after reaching a certain level, would take off. This prediction turned out to be half right.

In retrospect there were a number of difficulties or mistakes in the Picturephone® debacle. Some people say the price was too high, or that the black-and-white Picturephone came out at a time when people were expecting color, or that the resolution was too low. These observations are undoubtedly true, though probably in themselves not the reason for market failure. My own belief is that the Picturephone® offered too little benefit to human communications to justify the awkwardness and technological intrusiveness of the instrument.

The Picturephone® failed because the market—society's need—was seriously misjudged. It was a case not only of mechanically incorrect market projections, but of a lack of fundamental understanding of the true societal nature of communications. These issues are deep and murky, and not amenable to simple technological solutions. It even took the ordinary telephone several decades to gain acceptance from a wary public.

Home Information

The second example of misjudging societal needs and desires during the last decade is home information systems, introduced in many countries throughout the world. The Prestel system in the United Kingdom set a gleaming technological example. With an ordinary television set and an adapter for the existing telephone line, it was possible to get individualized information, such as stock prices, news and weather, sports, home shopping, banking, and so forth.

Technologists were fascinated with the possibilities of home information systems. Market trials were conducted in many countries in which selected customers in certain communities were given free service. Follow-up interviews and questionnaires were used to determine the market acceptance of the service. Most of these trials predicted glowing market acceptance and a willingness to pay about $10 per month per home.

So many conferences were devoted to the subject that, as the early market returns from actual paying service began to turn sour, one speaker quipped that the only people making money in this business were the ones running conferences. It seemed that people had said they wanted this service only while it was free. It was fun to be selected to be part of a trial, but paying real money for a service that was viewed as marginally useful was something else.

The ultimate success of home information is still questionable. It is likely that Prodigy and Compuserve and others in the business would argue hopefully that such services are becoming popular. But I suspect that most people in telecommunications outside of those with a vested interest would say that the acceptance by society of home information services has been far less than technologists hoped for or expected. The big exception to this generalization would be Minitel in France, where the government provided both planned vision and subsidy to put miniature computer terminals in millions of homes. The role of government in shaping this social information age crusade in France is a fascinating subject, and not unrelated to the topic at hand, but would take us to far astray from the current theme to be worth the trip.

Facsimile

Turning now to the two examples of social acceptance exceeding techno-logical expectation, let me first mention the facsimile machine. Surprisingly, versions were invented three or four decades ago. We can remember the "wire photos" of the newspapers, for example. Yet no one seemed to appreciate the value for ordinary business dealings until the late 1980s. Several things happened about that time. Technology, and Japanese manufacturing skills, had reached a point where a good-quality fax machine cost roughly $1,000—a level at which middle-level business managers could justify, and perhaps more importantly, could authorize, the purchase of a machine.

Reaching a price threshold is a familiar technological achievement, but other factors may have been more responsible for the fax machine's success. This was shortly after the time that Federal Express had created from almost nothing the appreciation of the value of time in the delivery of written material. As the advertisement said, "When it positively, absolutely has to be there overnight." Suddenly, time mattered. Thus it may be that fax rode on the crest of a social revolution fostered by overnight delivery services.

Another important element in the facsimile revolution was the role of standards in both codifying and shaping societal needs. As long as your own fax machine could talk only to an exact mate produced by the same manufacturer, the usage was minimal. International standardization opened the door to cross-usage, multiplied the power of individual machines, and provided the boost that carried the usage over a critical threshold of universal acceptance.

Today standards are preeminently important in telecommunications. Often, as it happened so often in the past, new standards only certify what has become a de facto guide because of market dominance, but more and more of today's standards lead the market. Perhaps the round tables where parties meet to determine standards are a modern, parliamentary equivalent of that Ouija board.

Cellular Telephony

The final example of societal interplay from telecommunications is the cellular telephone. A new form of high-capacity mobile telephony was con-ceived from basic principles during the early 1970s. There was no market need that could be asserted to justify the need for orders of magnitude more mobile telephones. The market at that time was small and relatively stagnant. Opening up more mobile capacity was a gamble similar to building highways into swamps.

Federal policy arguments and decrees held up the spread of cellular telephony for years. It is not a happy tale, but issues of competition, fairness, and the role of government came to bear on this technology, as they have on other technologically inspired social innovations. Eventually, a form of competition was mandated and the base stations and mobile telephones began to be built in quantity. But how big was the market? One high-priced, in-depth market study was influential in predicting a very small market. Those that need car phones are a special, small segment of the population, the study said. They will buy cellular telephones regardless of price. No one else needs or wants such a telephone; thus there is no price sensitivity.

But these market predictions were completely wrong. This time society adopted the original technological dream. Society decided that the cellular phone was not the exclusive province of the rich or the enslaving tool of the traveling salesman, but rather a means of extending human networking and societal togetherness for the common person. The original architects of the cellular system must feel proud, even if the vagaries of government policy and the inexactness of marketing predictions have decided that the financial rewards would go elsewhere.

Lessons Learned

In each of these examples the technology was not so important per se as the societal acceptance of the technology. In some real sense the facsimile and the cellular telephone were *social* inventions rather than technological inventions. The primary way that society signaled this acceptance was through the economics of the marketplace, though we see that governmental action was significant in the cellular telephone and in the relative success of the Minitel in France. Government policy in an indirect way also influenced the Picturephone®, in that the development of this system was allowed as a part of the rate base for the telephone monopoly. Thus society, according to decisions of its government, funded the Picturephone®. When later it was given a more direct vote on this matter in the form of individual purchasing decisions, it decided against the product.

Other examples of technologically inspired social inventions are all about us. I consider the copy machine, personal stereos, music videos, ESPN, CNN, the *USA Today* newspaper, and even the plethora of video rental stores as social derivatives of technology. Many of these institutions have affected our lives in significant ways. Who would have believed 10 years ago that practically every commercial street in almost every little town in the country would have a video rental store? Certainly the engineers working to perfect the video tape recorder had no conception of how they would change society. Nor did the inventors of the optical disc have any thought that their technology would be used for *audio* recording (when it was so obviously intended for video), and would completely displace the long-playing vinyl records from the shelves of the world's stores.

The examples also show the frustrations in market predictions about how society will act in accepting or rejecting technology. Asking individuals, taking polls, conducting discussions with focus groups, running field trials, and other market studies seem regularly to fail. It seems to me that the information simply is not there to be uncovered prematurely. As in the Ouija board, what is required is a joint decision over a period of time by a great many people—people who are largely unaware that they are even contributing to the decision.

There seems to be no substitute for the market itself as an arbiter of societal taste. Thus engineers must dare to try. Some technology will fail, but sometimes the determined application of a technological dream—even a simple one—can forever change society for the better.

TRENDS IN THE SOCIOTECHNICAL SYSTEM

When we look at the great technology trends from the past, we see how they created social revolution. Technology made possible the industrial revolution, and in this century it is forging the information age. All around us now we see the deepening of this computer-inspired age of information. The heavy industries are languishing, while service industries proliferate. Computer networks enmesh the world, and the global village seems more a reality than a tired cliché. Computers are underfoot everywhere, and we are increasingly dependent upon them to keep our records and do what amounts to the bookkeeping for business. More and more information is coming on-line, and digital libraries are just around the corner.

When the industrial revolution made the mass production of standard goods possible, it also took away the freedom of choice. Computers in the information age promise to give us back our individuality. Not only will information itself be customized to the recipient, but through flexible, computerized manufacture we will be able to have large varieties of individualized products.

This deepening of the information age also brings a number of negative consequences. One of them is information overload. Computers are getting faster, but we humans are not changing in our fundamental ability to consume and produce information. Every day I feel this limitation more and more acutely. I cannot read all that is being produced that seems relevant to my work. The flood increases every day, but I read only at the same rate, and the number of hours in the day remains fixed.

In addition to information overload there is communications overload. The fax machine and the cellular telephone are examples; so is the rise of electronic mail, voice mail, telephone answering machines, cable television, phones in airplanes, pagers, and so forth. Being connected is wonderful, but being entwined is something else. It is easy to drown in the din of virtual junk mail being produced in the various broadcast and personalized media.

A fundamental residue of the information age is the increase in complexity— complexity of technological systems, of business systems, and of social systems.

They seem to demonstrate a form of the second law of thermodynamics. Entropy is always on the rise. We see this particularly in large-scale systems. The telephone network, for example, was easily understandable and manageable only a decade ago. Now it seems to have slipped past the comprehension of any single person. The collapse of a significant portion of the AT&T network on January 15, 1990, was a singular event that underlined a new vulnerability mired in complexity. The control software for an electronic switching center now comprises about two million lines of code. That in itself is overwhelming, but the true difficulty is that these switching centers are themselves networked on a higher level. In other words, they talk to each other.

Other large-scale, interconnected systems include transportation, the environment and the earth's ecosystem, the air traffic control system, and the strategic defense system. Many of these systems have to do with what we call infrastructure. It is a major problem of our day—while the traditional infrastructure seems to be crumbling, the emerging infrastructure is fraught with complexity. These new systems are all manifestations of the accumulation of unfathomable complexity permitted and encouraged by the information age. Perhaps the most important problem of our time is the management of complexity.

In his best-selling book *Megatrends*, John Naisbitt observed that the computer is a tool that manages complexity, and as such, just as highways encourage more cars, the computer invites more complexity into society. The question is whether the ability of computers to manage complexity can keep up with the concomitant increase in complexity. There is considerable hope, because one of the most important tools that computers bring is the ability to simulate. If we are able to make useful models of important social and technical systems, then the power of supercomputers may be brought to bear on sociotechnical problems, giving us new understanding and ability to manage our societal problems.

Computers also give us an enhanced ability to monitor and control our large social systems. An example is the vision of an intelligent vehicle highway system, where highway traffic is measured in individual detail, transmitted within a computer network, processed with respect to mathematical models, and used to regulate and control flows. Our infrastructure will also be aided by structural monitoring of bridges, buildings, and airframes. Certainly there will be rich opportunity for the application of artificial intelligence, particularly in the development of expert systems that are able to apply heuristics to these seemingly intractable problems.

The social and business systems have also been adapting to the information age. Intellectual property has become a new branch of law, and has contributed its own ambiguities to an increasingly litigious society. The financial system has new problems of stability and control, as exemplified by program trading and the increasing volatility of the market. Moreover, the savings and loan crisis has shown the vulnerability of the banking system. The time constants evolving in the economic system have also worked against the development of new science and technology, as business leaders have focused more and more on the short-term profitability rather than the long-term investment required for stable research.

THE FUTURE

What comes after the information age? Obviously, no one knows, but I could suggest two possibilities. One would be an age of wisdom, where the myriad details of information that are overwhelming us now became subsumed in a higher-level emphasis on ideas. I assume that computers will be given many human abilities, such as speech recognition, language understanding, and image understanding. They will be able to do the detailed work that now seems the province of humans. It seems a characteristic of the information age that we have become a nation of clerks. Millions of people work in front of a computer screen, reading extracted information and relaying it to someone else. Computers will take over these clerical jobs, freeing us for something more worthy of our human intellect. If and when this happens, technology will again have transformed the very fabric of society.

The other possibility I could foresee would be another age of renaissance—almost a turning away from technology. I spoke earlier of the basic distrust that much of society has for technology. It is getting worse; C. P. Snow's two cultures are drifting further apart. Half the nation works on computers, while the other half (a larger half, to be sure) cannot program their video tape recorders.

The increasing complexity of life is a worrisome thing to most people. A very small segment of society is equipped to deal with this complexity. Technology is widely viewed as responsible, and it is conceivable that there could be a movement away from technology—toward art, religion, music, and philosophical thought, for example. However, there is also the possibility of a negative movement. It is probably significant that the book *Everything I Needed to Know I Learned in Kindergarten* is a best-seller. It expresses a desire for simplicity, but in a form that seems to me to be regressive.

The simplicity that people so desire can be achieved through the application of higher-level technology, but it can also be achieved by the outright rejection of all that technology stands for. It is comforting to be told that you do not need to know anything about the complexities of the world, but I am afraid this is a self-defeating message. I believe that we are going through a difficult period in terms of both increasing complexity and decay of the infrastructure. I believe that technology will offer solutions, but what do I know; I am only an engineer.

Appendixes

Appendix A
Tribute to J. Herbert Hollomon

ROLAND W. SCHMITT

I am more than pleased at the opportunity to make a few opening remarks about the person to whom this symposium is dedicated—J. Herbert Hollomon. Herb Hollomon inspired the founding of this Academy, so, in a way, he has touched the lives of all of us here today. The topic and the speakers of this symposium could not be more appropriate to his memory—they represent values and interests that he deeply held; he would truly relish the scope, the depth and the vision of today's speakers though I am sure he would also lay down a fiery challenge to each of them as he always did to those around him.

But the reason I feel especially privileged in making these remarks is that I am one of many whose lives were changed—profoundly and fundamentally—by Herb Hollomon. I dare say there are quite a few others in the audience who could say the same thing, so I am pleased to represent them. I am going to skip the conventional biographical details and go straight to some of my very personal views of this man.

To begin with, he tricked me and lured me into management—and I mean that literally. His first foray was to ask me to manage a group for only six months while the regular manager was on a special assignment. I remember walking away from that session wondering why he thought so little of my research

And then having enticed me into a job I did not want, he proceeded to teach me that it was a job I did not understand. "Good managers," Herb said, "work for the people in their organization, not vice versa." "And good managers," he said, "try to hire only people who are better than they are." Like so many of the things that Herb espoused, these are powerful oversimplifications that

101

pushed the limits of plausibility, that were partially true, and that Herb himself partially practiced.

"Be sure you don't compete with your own people," he would also say. But he taught me that it was okay to tamper in people's research, even basic research —something I did not exactly learn in academia! There was the time that he wanted me to get a member of my group to change his area of research, even though this person was regularly publishing very good work. I argued, "Suppose some misguided manager had made Faraday change his research from electricity to paraffin;" "Nonsense," said Herb, "Faraday would then have revolutionized both organic and physical chemistry." So I set about to induce the change, and Herb was right; soon the person was doing work of even better quality in an area of more interest to us.

One memory that I am sure everyone who worked with Herb has is of plenty of laughter. Working with him was fun, and around him you could be serious without taking yourself too seriously.

At this time in the late 1940s and 1950s Herb Hollomon was building a research group in the vanguard of the interdisciplinary approach to materials. Kurt Vonnegut, who has since become a famous novelist but who was then writing news releases for the General Electric Research Laboratory, said about Herb that "he feels that tradition . . . and hunches still guide metallurgy . . . for lack of a basic, scientific understanding of the processes that make metals behave as they do." And, Vonnegut said, Hollomon wanted to " take the guesswork and witchcraft out of one of the oldest fields known to mankind." It was the hey-day of the linear theory of innovation—going from basic research to invention to application and use—and Herb at that time was not only a proponent but a leading practitioner. He organized his group of 125 or so scientists and engineers into sections devoted to basic research, to invention, and to development; innovative breakthroughs were supposed to march through this assembly line and on to profits for General Electric.

Now whatever else might be said, there is no doubt about the scientific and technical impact of the group that Herb assembled in the 1950s. For example, the people who joined the group and worked in it during that period produced one Nobel Laureate and 17 memberships in the National Academies of Engineering and Sciences. The linear process of innovation, as everyone knows today—in hindsight—has its problems. But they were not as clear then, and it was an exciting time to be trying.

In any event, Herb Hollomon's style would not tolerate the paralysis of uncertainty—he always pushed ahead through any thickets of doubt or error. And like Brer Rabbit in the briar patch, he always emerged winning in one way or another because there were always visions and ideas that Herb pumped into and out of those around him.

To be around Herb Hollomon was to be constantly challenged—pressed to the limits of your own ability, intellect, skill, self-confidence, fortitude, diplomacy, patience, and even privacy. He was always all over you as a person—wanting to know everything—and I mean everything. For example, when I became engaged, I still remember being grilled about why I had given a ruby and a painting instead of the conventional diamond to the lady! But, what might have been intrusive curiosity in another person was commitment in Hollomon—commitment to you, to what you were, to what you might become, to what you could do to change the world. I did not see him often in later years, after his stroke—but when I did, the biggest and saddest change other than the paralysis itself was that even with his still-undiluted intensity about the world, his interest in your personal affairs no longer burned as brightly. To me it was the signal of how devastating his paralysis was.

So, the man to whom this symposium is dedicated ranged through the breadth and depth of human interests and emotions as energetically and profoundly as anyone could. He made things happen; to individuals, to institutions, to our nation, to the world. This is a fitting occasion to honor his memory.

Appendix B
Engineering's Great Challenge—The 1960s

J. HERBERT HOLLOMON

Throughout the nation, speakers like myself are commemorating National Engineers Week by giving their views of the great challenges facing engineering. My recent association with engineering has been brief. I came to General Electric's General Engineering Laboratory less than a month ago, drawn, in part, by the challenges facing us and our society. Thus, I turn my attention from science to engineering—from understanding to doing. Having had so little time to examine the details of current engineering problems, I was afraid and almost unwilling to describe the challenges, or prescribe how you and I might meet them. However, the consequences of our failure to overcome the ones I do see are so great, I have the temerity to try to tell you about them—and to encourage young men and women to grid for the fray.

Recent years have seen remarkable changes in our way of life—in our wealth, in our reduced supply of national resources, in our relative economic and military power, and in the aspirations of the poorer peoples of the world.

TECHNOLOGICAL EXPANSION

We have seen the fruits of nuclear research as fission and fusion atomic bombs. We engineered the first nuclear-powered submarine and "sailed" it under

This paper was presented at a joint meeting of regional engineering groups commemorating National Engineers Week, Schenectady, New York, 23 February 1960. Dr. Hollomon was at that time director of General Electric's General Engineering Laboratory in Schenectady.

the North Pole—a triumph of our ability to guide man without seeing the stars. Supersonic flight became a reality, and jet-powered aircraft make four-hour trips to the West Coast. Television viewing became a national pastime and its industry so important that Congress has undertaken to investigate it. Changes came at such a rapid pace that tranquilizers, unknown before 1954, have more than 20 million jittery users today.

Research in medicine has had dramatic consequences. Infectious diseases have been brought under control by antibiotics. The vaccines promise to eliminate crippling polio. Research on cancer and heart disease give promise of eliminating these great killers, bringing to man more than his three score and ten, with the attendant problems of an aging people and the population explosion in Asia, Africa, and South America—and a public debate on birth control.

The mechanization of industry largely through the use of electric power has lightened our work load and given us the leisure to enjoy all manner of recreation—and created new industries to satisfy our senses.

PLANNED INNOVATION

These great changes have come largely from a new resource only recently discovered and not yet understood or controlled—from research and development—from science and modern engineering. We are learning how to produce innovation—change—progress—at will. The process portends a way of life as revolutionary as the concept of the importance and dignity of man that wrought the Renaissance, and as forceful as the concept of capital formation that initiated the industrial revolution.

From the birth of our country on July 4, 1776, until today, February 23, 1960, a total of $108 billion has been spent on research and development in this country. Half of these expenditures were made since February 5, 1955—a scant five years ago. We have spent as much money on research and development in the last five years—$54 billion—as was spent in the 178 years between the signing of the Declaration of Independence and the first use of tranquilizers! The amount predicted to be spent in the single year 1960 is $15 billion.

If this accelerating activity is to serve society and fulfill man's dreams, we must learn to use it to his benefit and to prevent the devastation of its uncontrolled consequence.

This is a challenge of great moment.

What are the problems that our new world faces?

We are constantly reminded of the general destruction possible from the use of atomic weapons. Adequate means of monitoring and detecting atomic explosions might make possible agreement between the great powers and the control of nuclear weapons.

OPPORTUNITIES FOR ENGINEERS

The growing population and the mechanization of industry have produced hugh urban centers—one, for example, extends from Boston to Norfolk—with all their problems. We can fly from New York City to San Francisco in about four hours but have difficulty in making the trip from New York to Long Island in the same time. Air pollution in some cities is so extreme that it threatens public health. Water, in some areas, is so scarce that an artificial and economic means of recovering it from the sea is imperative. The growth of the cities has created such housing problems that many of our people live in horrible slums.

Engineers will design computers that will think like men—and faster—and relieve us from laborious mental tasks. They will make possible rational control of vast enterprises. The impact of this automation has already begun to affect labor relations, as in the recent steel strike, and will radically change our industrial labor system.

In recent years, Europeans and Japanese, recovering from postwar devastation with American aid, have seemed to use the new technology faster and more effectively than have we. As a result of the low cost of their labor and the speed with which they engineer new products, they have begun to threaten some of American industry with foreign competition.

To meet this competition is another challenge of engineering.

To the astonishment of the world Russia built the hydrogen bomb years sooner than we predicted, and we blamed it on spies. She then launched the space age and, in the eyes of the rest of the world, toppled Uncle Sam from his pedestal of technological superiority—and with a satellite larger than we've been able to launch years later. The Russian intercontinental ballistic missile deposed the American bomber from its prime position as the final strategic weapon. The consequent lag in defense is still a subject for national argument and is a challenge to the management of engineering.

The Russians not only recovered from a devastating war, exploded hydrogen bombs, built space ships, constructed a modern steel industry and an electric power system, educated vast numbers of engineers dedicated to their society, but also gave a dream to the world's poor and the exploited of a new and prosperous world that competes with the American idyl.

The great masses of Africa, Asia, and South America, seeing our planes and our prosperous people and hearing our radio, cry out for a "place in the sun." They are jealous of our wealth and our luxuries and resent our air of superiority. Their problem is to build a new world using the tools of modern technology, but tuned to their needs and to their conditions—a dam at Aswan, a steel mill for India, bricks for Africa, insecticides for Indochina, tools for Argentina. To do these things requires an understanding of modern engineering and a supply of the capital of trained people that the poor cannot yet afford—and which we must furnish.

These people and their aspirations present new problems to be solved and new engineering to be done. From all sides there are cries for financial and engineering help to meet the needs of their people. These are cries first for survival, then for political, cultural and religious opportunity.

WHO CAN BEST MEET THE CHALLENGE?

And with their appreciation of technology and their dramatic demonstration of technical achievements, the Russians are convincing these people that the Soviet Union can better meet their needs and support their aspirations than can the West.

Khrushchev has said that Russia intends to defeat us in peaceful competition. It is not only a competition in aid and advice to the underdeveloped countries but a competition in trade. America will face products made with Russian labor paid about one-tenth as much as ours and with prices controlled by the state. As a recent American visitor comments, "A strange thought crosses your mind: a future Russia emerging from the Iron Curtain, and America withdrawing behind the Dollar Curtain, priced out of the market, left trading with itself. 'Could it be?' you ask yourself."

When I was in Russia, I asked as many people as I could to tell me of their dreams. A typical answer was: "To build a free and peaceful world where people may be happy and prosperous and express the highest aspirations of man."

And this too, is a challenge. But do all these challenge engineering? Many of these great changes of our time have come directly from science—from new discoveries about nature. These direct applications of science and the vast research and development have confused the primary roles of science and engineering. The success of the missile firing is announced, according to the papers, by a "scientist" and the failure is a failure of science.

Historically, the translation of scientific discovery to use has taken decades. The steam engine and the airplane were developed from principles of mechanics long known to scientists. Steinmetz and Edison used principles of electricity proved valid years before to found the electrical industry. On the other hand, the results of nuclear physics were almost directly applied to the construction of a self-sustaining nuclear reactor, to atomic bombs, and to nuclear electric power stations. A new discovery of the behavior of solids led to the transistor, a new miniature electronic device—a solid vacuum tube. Both of these developments were direct but unanticipated and unpredicted contributions to society from science. In order to create and be alert to the exceptional, useful consequences of discovery in science, industry has created scientific research laboratories such as ours at the Knolls.

These advances and others like them have led people to think of science in terms of its applications, playing the role of satisfying man's needs. The prime and unique purpose of science, that of seeking knowledge and understanding for its own sake, is diluted and the only vehicle for satisfying man's curiosity about his world is damaged. Engineering, whose primary purpose is to satisfy man's needs and meet the physical challenges of his world, is eclipsed. The engineer uses art and science to make matter and power useful to man.

To call both of these key activities by the same name dilutes both to the disadvantage of each. Young men and women willing to dedicate themselves to the service of man in either learning or doing science or engineering have no clear call to service.

Professor Morgan of Yale reminds us that the search for truth is a revolutionary activity. "The search for it again and again overturned beliefs of long standing, in science, in religion, and in politics." To commit science to solving utilitarian problems will threaten free inquiry and destroy the seeds of innovation that may alter the direction of human life.

ROLE OF ENGINEERING NOT RECOGNIZED

The failure to recognize the role of engineering likewise makes it difficult to attract young people to a great human activity, to get the job done, to build the rockets now, using the available resources without waiting for the next bit of scientific discovery, to build the bridges when they're needed, to make the tools to heal the sick, and to go to the moon. It is the job of engineering to devise the means of feeding, housing, and protecting society, of improving the means of communication and transportation, of meeting the challenges of space, of exploiting automation, and of helping underprivileged people.

It is to these challenges that engineering should direct itself.

To meet such challenges in these times will require changes in the whole of engineering. Modern science generates new knowledge so rapidly that the education of engineers must be deepened and broadened to appreciate and use it, and yet not become all science without focus on society. Already the electrical engineer, for example, is likely to be concerned with the structure of crystals and the role of computers in industrial operations. The civil engineer must understand both the potentialities of data processing and the complexities of radioactive waste disposal. The mechanical engineer is confronted with the need for machines which operate at both temperatures near absolute zero and those of man-made suns.

This rapid advance and this complexity are causing drastic changes in engineering education. Within a few years advanced training will be required of all engineers, and ways will have to be found to continue their education throughout their careers so that they can effectively use the new science to serve society. It is the responsibility of engineering to create from science the new tools—to develop the new technology—just as it is the responsibility of science to show the way for its first use.

To use the new technology will also require research—research aimed at adding that information and understanding needed to get the job done. The engineering of rockets demands information about high temperature materials— about gyros—and about high vacua. The development of computers needs to be based on information, derived from engineering, on the behavior of complex electronic systems and of semiconductor devices. The requirements of modern man as well as his curiosity stimulate investigation.

To be a professional engineer and to attract young people to this great calling, it is not enough, though important, to gather together in engineering societies and associations. A professional is one who feels a personal and individual sense of responsibility of dedication.

RESPONSIBILITY OF THE INDIVIDUAL

Each of us must explore the role of engineering and assume individual responsibility for high performance and excellence. We must come to understand science, its importance to society and to support it and use it.

We can take a personal interest in community engineering problems—in city planning, in slum clearance, and in water pollution.

We can even attack international problems without waiting for the government. Here at home, some two dozen technical people, realizing their responsibilities to society and, incidentally, having fun doing it, have formed the MASE Technical Consultation Committee. They are offering technical assistance to underdeveloped countries—and on their own time. They perform four kinds of services. They prepare reports on engineering requirements such as that on solar cooking for Iran; they develop specific devices, as a methane-burning refrigerator for Brazil; they answer questions like that from a missionary in Peru interested in the operation of suction pumps at high altitudes; and they help various foreign groups find out about similar problems in other countries. Here is the American spirit at its best.

NATIONAL ACADEMY OF ENGINEERING

But the work of individuals and of the professional societies is still not enough to clarify the role of engineering, make it more effective in our national life, or attract young people to it.

I, therefore, propose that a National Academy of Engineering be established through an act of Congress. It would consist of several hundred engineers. The Academy should be analogous to the National Academy of Sciences which was set up by Congress and approved by President Lincoln in 1863, another time of ferment. The National Academy of Sciences, though representing both science and engineering at the highest level of government, has only about 10 percent of its members with background in engineering, and the role of engineering is submerged or obscured.

The charter of this new academy would direct that it shall, whenever called upon by any department of the government, investigate, examine, experiment, and report upon any subject of engineering. A National Engineering Council would be established as a principal agency of the new Academy of Engineering. This council would be charged with promoting engineering and encouraging the application and dissemination of engineering information, using where possible the present professional and technical societies. Neither the Academy nor the Council would control engineering or industry, but together they would permit the assembly of the best engineering advice for national affairs, and would strengthen the unity of purpose that engineering and engineering societies are establishing. The Academy would represent and honor the million engineers of our country.

BENEFITS TO SCIENCE AND ENGINEERING

This Academy of Engineering would strengthen and benefit both science and engineering so that they, like Damon and Phythias, would stand and aid each other and thereby better serve the nation.

Let me now quote from Semonov of the Academy of Sciences of the U.S.S.R.: "The power of contemporary science and technology is such that they can, in principle, provide the highest level of well-being for all people on the globe. But capitalist society is organically incapable, by virtue of private vested interests, of fixing this goal as an organized aim of society and state."

I believe that engineers will not fail to accept this supreme challenge to our way of life. We—you and I—must meet it.

Contributors

ROBERT McCORMICK ADAMS is secretary of the Smithsonian Institution in Washington, D.C., and a member of the National Academy of Sciences. Dr. Adams is a scholar of Middle East urban and agricultural history, comparative early civilizations (Mesopotamia and Mexico), history of technology, and science and higher education policies. At the University of Chicago he served as Distinguished Service Professor, director of the Oriental Institute, dean of social sciences, and provost. He holds a doctorate in anthropology from the University of Chicago. Address: Smithsonian Institution, 1000 Jefferson Drive, S.W., Washington, D.C. 20560.

GEORGE BUGLIARELLO is president of Polytechnic University and a member of the National Academy of Engineering. Dr. Bugliarello is an educator with a broad background ranging from civil engineering to computer languages, biomedical engineering and fluid mechanics. He currently chairs Metrotech Corporation established by the university to create an industry park in New York City. He is founder and editor of *Technology in Society*, an international journal, and author of more than 200 professional papers and numerous books. He received a doctorate degree in engineering from the Massachusetts Institute of Technology. Address: Polytechnic University, 333 Jay Street, Brooklyn, New York 11201.

JOHN W. FAIRCLOUGH is chairman of the Centre for the Exploitation of Science and Technology, chairman of Rothschild Ventures Ltd., chairman of the United Kingdom Engineering Council, and a foreign associate of the National Academy of Engineering. From 1986 to 1990 he served as chief scientific adviser to the Cabinet Office, London, England after a distinguished industrial career at IBM that spanned over 30 years. At IBM he started as a project engineer and went on to become laboratory director and director of marketing and data services, vice president of communication systems and, in 1983, director of manufacturing and development and chairman of IBM's United Kingdom Laboratories. He holds an electrical engineering degree from Manchester University. Address: The Old Blue Boar, 25 St. Johns Street, Winchester S0238HF, United Kingdom.

THOMAS P. HUGHES is Mellon Professor of the History and Sociology of Science at the University of Pennsylvania. He holds the Torsten Althin Chair in History of Technology and Society at the Swedish Royal Institute of Technology and is a foreign member of the Royal Swedish Academy of Engineering Sciences. He has written extensively about American and European history with special attention to technological and social change. His most recent books include *American Genesis: A Century of Invention and Technological Enthusiasm (1870–1970)*, a Pulitzer Prize finalist in history in 1990, and *Lewis Mumford: Public Intellectual*, coedited with Agatha Hughes. Address: Department of History and Sociology of Science, E. F. Smith Hall D6, University of Pennsylvania, Philadelphia, Pennsylvania 19104.

ROBERT W. LUCKY is executive director of Research Communications Sciences Division of AT&T Bell Laboratories and a member of the National Academy of Engineering. Dr. Lucky's division does research on methods and technologies for future communication and computing, including current emphasis on lightwave systems, multiprocessor computer systems, robotics, artificial intelligence, and new physical devices for optics and electronics. He is best known for his work at AT&T on the invention of the adaptive equalizer—a technique used in all high-speed data transmission for correcting distortion in telephone signals. His textbook *Principles of Data Communication* has been a recognized standard in its field and his most recent written work is a semitechnical book entitled *Silicon Dreams*, published last year. He received a doctorate in electrical engineering from Purdue University. Address: AT&T Bell Laboratories, Crawfords Corner Road, Room 4E-605, Holmdel, New Jersey 07733-1988.

HEDY E. SLADOVICH was a research associate with the National Academy of Engineering Program Office from 1988 to 1991. Before joining the Technology and Environment Program at the Academy, she worked as a researcher for the National Geographic Society, as a biotechnology analyst with E. F. Hutton, and as a field ecologist with the Ecosystems Center of the Marine Biological Laboratory in Woods Hole, Massachusetts. Her interests revolve around the interactions of technology, society, and environment. Ms. Sladovich received her bachelor's degree in biology and physiological psychology from Oakland

University and did graduate work in science policy and international affairs at George Washington University.

WALTER G. VINCENTI (Symposium Chair) is professor emeritus of Aeronautics and Astronautics at Stanford University and a member of the National Academy of Engineering. He has made significant contributions to the experimental and theoretical understanding of transonic, supersonic, and high-temperature gas flows and to study of the history of technology. His books include *Introduction to Physical Gas Dynamics* with C. H. Kruger, *The Britannia Bridge: The Generation and Diffusion of Technological Knowledge* with Nathan Rosenberg, and *What Engineers Know and How They Know It.* Address: 13200 E. Sunset Drive, Los Altos Hills, California 94022.

MARINA v.N. WHITMAN is Vice President and Group Executive, Public Affairs and Marketing Group at General Motors. Dr. Whitman is an economist with broad experience in academic, governmental, and private advisory organizations concerned with domestic and international economic issues. She is author of *Reflections on Interdependence,* a book that explores the impact on U.S. foreign economic policy of growing mutual economic dependence of nations since the end of World War II, and a monograph entitled *International Trade and Investment: Two Perspectives* that relates patterns of international production, trade, and investment in the automobile industry to patterns predicted on the basis of economic theory. She holds a doctorate degree in economics from Columbia University. Address: Public Affairs Group, General Motors Corporation, 3044 W. Grand Boulevard, Detroit, Michigan 48202.